When we submit our lives to what we read in Scripture, we find that we're being led not to see God in our stories but to see our stories in God's. God is the larger context and plot in which our stories find themselves.

EUGENE H. PETERSON

The INVITATION

The INVITATION

A SIMPLE GUIDE TO THE BIBLE

EUGENE H. PETERSON

OUR GUARANTEE TO YOU

We believe so strongly in the message of our books that we are making this quality guarantee to you. If for any reason you are disappointed with the content of this book, return the title page to us with your name and address and we will refund to you the list price of the book. To help us serve you better, please briefly describe why you were disappointed. Mail your refund request to: NavPress, P.O. Box 35002, Colorado Springs, CO 80935.

For a free catalog
of NavPress books & Bible studies call
1-800-366-7788 (USA) or 1-800-839-4769 (Canada).

www.navpress.com

The Navigators is an international Christian organization. Our mission is to advance the gospel of Jesus and His kingdom into the nations through spiritual generations of laborers living and discipling among the lost. We see a vital movement of the gospel, fueled by prevailing prayer, flowing freely through relational networks and out into the nations where workers for the kingdom are next door to everywhere.

NavPress is the publishing ministry of The Navigators. The mission of NavPress is to reach, disciple, and equip people to know Christ and make Him known by publishing life-related materials that are biblically rooted and culturally relevant. Our vision is to stimulate spiritual transformation through every product we publish.

ISBN-13: 978-1-60006-233-9
ISBN-10: 1-60006-233-4

Cover design by www.studiogearbox.com
Cover image by Nicholas Belton
Creative Team: Dan Benson, Mary McNeil, Lori Mitchell, Darla Hightower, Arvid Wallen, Kathy Guist

Unless otherwise identified, all Scripture quotations in this publication are taken from *THE MESSAGE* (MSG). Copyright © 1993, 1994, 1995, 1996, 2000, 2001, 2002, 2005. Used by permission of NavPress Publishing Group.

"On Reading the Scriptures" compiled from Eugene H. Peterson, *Eat This Book* (Grand Rapids, MI: Eerdmans). Used by permission.

A special thanks to the International Bible Society for permission to include an edited version of the Bible notes The Drama of the Bible® 2002 by International Bible Society®. Used by permission. All rights reserved worldwide.

**Published in association with the literary agency of Alive Communications, Inc.,
7680 Goddard St., Suite 200, Colorado Springs, CO 80920.**

Library of Congress Cataloging-in-Publication Data
Peterson, Eugene H., 1932-
The invitation : a simple guide to the Bible / Eugene H. Peterson.
    p. cm.
  ISBN 978-1-60006-233-9
  1. Bible--Reading. 2. Bible--Study and teaching. 3. Bible--Criticism, interpretation, etc. I. Title.
BS617.P48 2008
220.6'1--dc22

                    2007033178

Printed in the United States of America

1 2 3 4 5 6 7 8 / 12 11 10 09 08

Contents

On Reading the Scriptures

In order to read the Scriptures adequately and accurately, it's necessary at the same time to live them. Not to live them as a prerequisite to reading them, and not to live them as a consequence of reading them, but to live them as we read them.

Reading the Scriptures isn't an activity discrete from living the gospel; it is integral to it. It means letting another have a say in everything we're saying and doing. It's as easy as that. And as hard.

This kind of reading has been named by our ancestors as *lectio divina*, often translated "spiritual reading." It means not only reading the text but also meditating on the text, praying the text, and living the text. It is reading that enters our souls the way food enters our stomachs, spreads through our blood, and transforms us. Christians don't simply learn or study or use Scripture; we feed on it. We assimilate it, taking it into our lives in such a way that it gets metabolized into acts of love, cups of cold water, missions into all the world, healing and evangelism and justice in Jesus' name, hands raised in adoration of the Father, feet washed in the company of the Son.

Words spoken and listened to, written and read are intended to do something in us, to give us health and wholeness, vitality and holiness, wisdom and hope.

We open this book and find that on page after page it takes us off guard, surprises us, and draws us into its reality, pulls us into participation with God on his terms.

My task is to bring into awareness that the biblical text, in the course of revealing God, pulls us into the revelation and welcomes us as participants in it. What I want to call attention to is that the Bible, all of it, is livable. It is, in fact, the text for living our lives.

The Scriptures not only reveal everything of who God is but also everything of who we are. And this revelation is done in such a way as to invite participation on both sides, of author and reader.

This may be the single most important thing to know as we come to read and study and believe these Holy Scriptures: this rich, alive, personally revealing God as experienced in Father, Son, and Holy Spirit, personally addressing us in whatever circumstances we find ourselves, at whatever age we are, in whatever state we are — me, you, us. Christian reading is participatory reading, receiving the words in such a way that they become interior to our lives, the rhythms and images becoming practices of prayer, acts of obedience, ways of love.

Holy Scripture is like fenced-in acreage, with rows of words and sentences that form rhythms in which we, the readers, participate but don't control. We meditatively enter this world of words and give obedient and glad assent. We submit our lives to this text so that God's will may be done on earth as it is in heaven.

Story is the primary verbal means of bringing God's Word to us. For that we can be most grateful, for story is our most accessible form of speech. But there's another reason for the appropriateness of story as a means of bringing God's Word. Story doesn't just tell us something and leave it there; it invites our participation. A good storyteller gathers us into the story. We feel the emotions, get caught up in the drama, identify with the characters, see into the nooks and crannies of life that we had overlooked, realize that there's more to this business of being human than we had yet explored. If the story is good, doors and windows open. Honest stories respect our freedom; they don't manipulate us, don't force us, don't distract us from life. They bring us into the spacious world in which God creates and saves and blesses. First through our imaginations and then through faith — imagination and faith are close kin — they offer us a place in the story, invite us into this large story that takes place under the broad skies of God's purposes.

One of the characteristic marks of the biblical storytellers is a certain reticence. There's an austere, spare quality to their stories. They don't tell us too much. They leave a lot of blanks in the narration, an implicit invitation to enter the story ourselves, just as we are, and to discover for ourselves how to fit in.

Stories suffer misinterpretation when we don't submit to them simply as stories. We're caught off guard when divine revelation arrives in such ordinary garb, and we mistakenly think it's our job to dress it up in the latest Paris-silk gown of theology, or to outfit it in a sturdy three-piece suit of ethics before we can deal with it. The simple, or not so simple, story is soon, like David under Saul's armor, so encumbered with moral admonitions, theological constructs, and scholarly debates that it can hardly move. There are, of course, always moral, theological, and historical elements in these stories that need to be studied, but never in dismissal of the story that is being told.

One of the many welcome consequences in learning to "read" our lives into the lives of Abraham and Sarah, Moses and Miriam, Hannah and Samuel, Ruth and David, Isaiah and Esther, Mary and Martha, Peter and Paul is a sense of affirmation and freedom; we don't have to fit into prefabricated moral or mental or religious boxes before we're admitted into the company of God. We're taken seriously, just as we are, and given a place in his story. For it is, after all, his story; none of us is the leading character in the story of our life.

Spiritual theology, using Scripture as text, doesn't present us with a moral code and tell us, "Live up to this"; nor does it set out a system of doctrine and say, "Think like this and you will live well." The biblical way is to tell a story and, in the telling, to invite us to "Live into this." This is what it looks like to be human in this God-made and God-ruled world; this is what is involved in becoming a human being and maturing as one.

When we submit our lives to what we read in Scripture, we find that we're being led not to see God in our stories but to see our stories in God's. God is the larger context and plot in which our stories find themselves.

The story that locates us in the large world of God and enlists us in following Jesus is told sentence by sentence. Walking and following, for the most part, don't require deliberate thought; they employ conditioned reflexes, muscle and nerve coordination acquired in the first few years of life. We walk without having to think about putting one step before another. We read a story the same way; the sentences unfold one after the other without our having to stop and ponder each period or verb tense.

But just as in walking without thinking, we sometimes miss important details in the terrain — flowers and rocks, for example — so in reading without thinking, we sometimes miss important details in the text. As we follow Jesus in making our way through this story, we find ourselves in the story.

But in finding some things, we overlook other things. We find ourselves from time to time stopping, or being stopped, and noticing details that make up the story. We attend to language the way a naturalist attends to flowers or a geologist attends to rocks. And we discover that words are never mere words — they convey spirit, meaning, energy, and truth. This is the work of exegesis, a technical term for carefully studying the text and listening to it rightly and well.

Careful study is necessary. Without study, spirituality becomes sappy. Without spirituality, study becomes self-indulgent. And without the two walking together, prayer ends up limping along in sighs and stutters.

Exegesis is necessary because we have a written word to attend to. It's God's Word, or so we believe, and we had better get it right. Exegesis is foundational to Christian spirituality. Foundations disappear from view as a building is constructed, but if the builders don't build a solid foundation, the building doesn't last long.

Too many Bible readers assume that exegesis is what you do after you've learned Greek and Hebrew. That's simply not true. Exegesis is nothing more than a careful and loving reading of the text in our mother tongue. Greek and Hebrew are well worth learning, but if you haven't had the privilege, settle for English. Once we learn to love this

text and bring a disciplined intelligence to it, we won't be far behind
the very best Greek and Hebrew scholars. Appreciate the learned
Scripture scholars, but don't be intimidated by them.
Exegesis is the furthest thing from an impersonal act of scholarship; it is an intensely personal act of love. It loves the one who speaks
the words enough to want to get them right. Exegesis is loving God
enough to stop and listen carefully to what he says. It follows that we
bring the leisure and attentiveness of lovers to this text, cherishing
every comma and semicolon, relishing the oddness of this preposi-
tion, delighting in the surprising placement of this noun. Lovers don't
take a quick look, get a "message" or a "meaning," and then run off
and talk endlessly with their friends about how they feel.

Exegesis doesn't mean mastering the text; it means submitting
to it as it is given to us. Exegesis doesn't take charge of the text and
impose superior knowledge on it; it enters the world of the text and
lets the text "read" us. Exegesis is an act of sustained humility.

If the knowledge we acquire through our reading and study of this
text diverts us from the very Jesus we started out following, we would
have been better off never to have opened the book in the first place.

The story gives form to sentences; the sentences provide content to
the story. Following Jesus requires that they hold together, thoroughly
integrated. Without the story, the sentences in the Bible — the Bible
verses — function as an encyclopedia of information from which we
select whatever we need at the moment. Without the precisely crafted
sentences, the story gets edited and revised by seductive suggestions
from some and by bullying urgencies from others, none of whom seem
to have much interest in following Jesus. But it was to make us followers of Jesus that this text was given to us in the first place, and if either
the large story or the detailed sentences are ever used for anything
else, however admirable or enticing, why bother?

The Bible of Surprises

Reading is the first thing, just reading the Bible. As we read we enter a new world of words and find ourselves in on a conversation in which God has the first and last words. We soon realize that we are included in the conversation. We didn't expect this. But this is precisely what generation after generation of Bible readers do find: The Bible is not only written about us but to us. In these pages we become insiders to a conversation in which God uses words to form and bless us, to teach and guide us, to forgive and save us.

"Hey there! All who are thirsty,
come to the water!
Are you penniless?
Come anyway — buy and eat!
Come, buy your drinks, buy wine and milk.
Buy without money — everything's free!
Why do you spend your money on junk food,
your hard-earned cash on cotton candy?
Listen to me, listen well: Eat only the best,
fill yourself with only the finest.
Pay attention, come close now,
listen carefully to my life-giving, life-nourishing words.
I'm making a lasting covenant commitment with you,
the same that I made with David: sure, solid, enduring love. . . ."

Seek God while he's here to be found,
pray to him while he's close at hand. (Isaiah 55:1-3,6)

We aren't used to this. We are used to reading books that explain things, or tell us what to do, or inspire or entertain us. But this is different. This is a world of revelation: God revealing to people just like us — men and women created in God's image — how God works and what is going on in this world in which we find ourselves. At the same time that God reveals all this, God draws us in by invitation and command to participate in God's working life. We gradually (or suddenly) realize that we are insiders in the most significant action of our time as God establishes his grand rule of love and justice on this earth (as it is in heaven). "Revelation" means that we are reading something we couldn't have guessed or figured out on our own. Revelation is what makes the Bible unique.

And so just reading the Bible and listening to what we read is the first thing. There will be time enough for study later on. But first, it is important simply to read, leisurely and thoughtfully. We need to get a feel for the way these stories and songs, these prayers and conversations, these sermons and visions, invite us into this large, large world in which the invisible God is behind and involved in everything visible and illuminates what it means to live here — really live, not just get across the street. As we read, and the longer we read, we begin to "get it" — we are in conversation with God. We find ourselves listening and answering in matters that most concern us: who we are, where we came from, where we are going, what makes us tick, the texture of the world and the communities we live in, and — most of all — the incredible love of God among us, doing for us what we cannot do for ourselves. Consider the best-known and most-beloved psalm:

> GOD, *my shepherd!*
> *I don't need a thing.*
> *You have bedded me down in lush meadows,*
> *you find me quiet pools to drink from.*

True to your word,
       you let me catch my breath
       and send me in the right direction.

Even when the way goes through
       Death Valley,
I'm not afraid
       when you walk at my side.
Your trusty shepherd's crook
       makes me feel secure.

You serve me a six-course dinner
       right in front of my enemies.
You revive my drooping head;
       my cup brims with blessing.

Your beauty and love chase after me
       every day of my life.
I'm back home in the house of GOD
       for the rest of my life. (Psalm 23)

Through reading the Bible, we see that there is far more to the world, more to us, more to what we see and more to what we don't see — more to everything! — than we had ever dreamed, and that this "more" has to do with God.

This is new for many of us, a different sort of book — a book that reads us even as we read it. We are used to picking up and reading books for what we can get out of them: information we can use, inspiration to energize us, instructions on how to do something or other, entertainment to while away a rainy day, wisdom that will guide us into living better. These things can and do take place when reading the Bible, but the Bible is given to us in the first place simply to invite us to make ourselves at home in the world of God, God's word and world, and become familiar with the way God speaks and the ways in which we answer him with our lives.

Our reading turns up some surprises. The biggest surprise for many is how accessible this book is to those who simply open it up and read it. Virtually anyone can read this Bible with understanding. The reason that new translations are made every couple of generations or so is to keep the language of the Bible current with the common speech we use, the very language in which it was first written. We don't have to be smart or well-educated to understand it, for it is written in the words and sentences we hear in the marketplace, on school playgrounds, and around the dinner table. Because the Bible is so famous and revered, many assume that we need experts to explain and interpret it for us — and, of course, there are some things that need to be explained. But the first men and women who listened to these words now written in our Bibles were ordinary, everyday, working-class people. One of the greatest of the early translators of the Bible into English, William Tyndale, said that he was translating so that "the boy that driveth the plough" would be able to read the Scriptures.

One well-educated African man, who later became one of the most influential Bible teachers in our history (Augustine), was greatly offended when he first read the Bible. Instead of a book cultivated and polished in the literary style he admired so much, he found it full of homespun, earthy stories of plain, unimportant people. He read it in a Latin translation full of slang and jargon. He took one look at what he considered the "unspiritual" quality of so many of its characters and the everydayness of Jesus, and contemptuously abandoned it. It was years before he realized that God had not taken the form of a sophisticated intellectual to teach us about highbrow heavenly culture so we could appreciate the finer things of God. When he saw that God entered our lives as a Jewish servant in order to save us from our sins, he started reading the Book gratefully and believingly.

Some are also surprised that Bible reading does not introduce us to a "nicer" world. This biblical world is decidedly not an ideal world, the kind we see advertised in travel posters. Suffering and injustice and ugliness are not purged from the world in which God works and loves and saves. Nothing is glossed over. God works patiently and deeply, but often in hidden ways, in the mess of our humanity and history. Ours is not a neat and tidy world in which we are assured that we can get everything under our control. This takes considerable getting used to — there is mystery everywhere. The Bible does not give us a predictable cause-effect world in which we can plan our careers and secure our futures. It is not a dream world in which everything works out according to our adolescent expectations; there is pain and poverty and abuse at which we cry out in indignation, "You can't let this happen!" For most of us it takes years and years and years to exchange our dream world for this real world of grace and mercy, sacrifice and love, freedom and joy — the God-saved world.

Yet another surprise is that the Bible does not flatter us. It is not trying to sell us anything that promises to make life easier. It doesn't offer secrets to what we often think of as prosperity or pleasure or high adventure. The reality that comes into focus as we read the Bible has to do with what God is doing in a saving love that includes us and everything we do. This is quite different from what our sin-stunted and culture-cluttered minds imagined. But our Bible reading does not give us access to a mail-order catalog of idols from which we can pick and choose to satisfy our fantasies. The Bible begins with God speaking creation and us into being. It continues with God entering into personalized and complex relationships with us, helping and blessing us, teaching and training us, correcting and disciplining us, loving and saving us. This is not an escape from reality but a plunge into more reality — a sacrificial but altogether better life all the way.

God doesn't force any of this on us: God's word is personal address, inviting, commanding, challenging, rebuking, judging, comforting, directing — but not forcing. Not coercing. We are given space and freedom to answer, to enter the conversation. For more than anything else the Bible invites our participation in the work and language of God.

As we read, we find that there is a connection between the Word Read and the Word Lived. Everything in this book is livable. Many of us find that the most important question we ask as we read is not "What does it mean?" but "How can I live it?" So we read personally, not impersonally. We read in order to live our true selves, not just get information that we can use to raise our standard of living. Bible reading is a means of listening to and obeying God, not gathering religious data by which we can be our own gods.

You are going to hear stories in this Book that will take you out of your preoccupation with yourself and into the spacious freedom in which God is working the world's salvation. You are going to come across words and sentences that stab you awake to a beauty and hope that will connect you with your real life.

Be sure to answer.

The Story of the Bible
in Five Acts

The heart and soul of the Bible is its story. It is the real saga of a particular people, how God called them and intended for them to bring blessing to all people.

Story is also the word that best describes our own lives. While we may or may not follow the right rules, investigate certain facts, and attempt to live wisely, none of these activities provides the central way we make sense of our lives. Stories give context and provide meaning.

All the different parts of the Bible come together as one narrative. To understand the Bible you must get to know its characters, understand its setting, and follow its plot.

The climax and ultimate resolution will make sense only if you've followed the earlier parts as a story. Learn to feel the tension and wrestle with its major conflict. Lose yourself in this story the way you do with a good novel.

We present here an abbreviated version of the story of the Bible as a drama in five acts.

Act I Creation

The drama begins with God already on the stage. He is creating the world. He makes a man, Adam, and places him in the Garden of Eden to work in it and take care of it. God's intention is for humanity to be in close relationship with him and in harmony with the rest of creation around them. God is described in these early chapters of the Bible as dwelling in the garden together with the first human beings, Adam and Eve. At the end of the first chapter of Genesis, God gives his own assessment of his work:

> *God looked over everything he had made; it was so good, so very good!*
> *(verse 31)*

Act I reveals God's desire for people and provides the setting for all the action that follows.

Act II The Fall

Tension is introduced in the story when Adam and Eve decide to go their own way and seek their own wisdom. They listen to the deceptive voice of God's enemy, Satan, and doubt God's trustworthiness. As a result of this rebellion:

> *God expelled them from the Garden of Eden and sent them to work the*
> *ground, the same dirt out of which they'd been made. He threw them out*
> *of the garden and stationed angel-cherubim and a revolving sword of fire*
> *east of it, guarding the path to the Tree-of-Life. (Genesis 3:23-24)*

God's intention in creation is known, but part of his own creation has put his plan off course. Can God regain his relationship with humanity and remove the curse from creation? Or did God's enemy effectively end the plan and subvert the story?

Acts I and II take only the first few pages in the Bible to be completed. Yet they introduce the struggle that dominates the rest of the story.

ACT III ISRAEL

GOD *told Abram: "Leave your country, your family, and your father's*
home for a land that I will show you. I'll make you a great nation and
bless you. I'll make you famous; you'll be a blessing. I'll bless those who
bless you; those who curse you I'll curse. All the families of the Earth
will be blessed through you." (Genesis 12:1-3)

In calling Abram (God later renamed him Abraham) and promising to make him into a great nation, God is narrowing his focus
and concentrating on one group of people for a period of time. But
the ultimate goal remains the same: to bless all the peoples on earth,
remove the curse from creation, and restore the original relationship
that existed in the garden.

When Abraham's descendants are later enslaved in Egypt, a central pattern in the story is set: God returns to his people, frees them,
and restores them to the land promised to them. God makes a covenant with this new nation of Israel at Mount Sinai. He appoints Moses
to be their leader during their liberation from Egypt — the Exodus. As
part of the covenant, God makes it clear that if his people remain true
to him and faithfully follow his ways, he will bless them in their new
land and make it like the original Garden of Eden.

However, if Israel is not faithful to the covenant, God warns them
that he will send them out of the land, just as he did with Adam and
Eve. Sadly, and in spite of God's repeated warnings and pleadings,
they are determined to go their own way. They break the covenant,
follow the false gods of the nations that surround them and bring the
judgment of God down upon themselves.

Abraham's descendants, chosen to reverse the failure of Adam,
have now apparently failed themselves. Along the way, however, God
has planted the seeds of a different outcome. One of Israel's kings,

David, is noted for being "a man after God's own heart." So God promises to send another king to Israel, a son of David, who will lead Israel wisely, bring the nation back to God and be the agent of blessing to the peoples of the world.

So while Act III ends tragically, with God apparently absent, the hope of a promise remains.

ACT IV JESUS

Four centuries later, the people of Israel are suffering under Roman occupation and waiting for God to return. An angel of God comes to a young woman named Mary and announces,

> *You will become pregnant and give birth to a son and call his name*
> *Jesus. He will be great, be called "Son of the Highest." The Lord God*
> *will give him the throne of his father David; He will rule Jacob's house*
> *forever — no end, ever, to his kingdom. (Luke 1:31-33)*

Jesus' arrival is introduced with the claim that God is keeping his promise.

So Jesus begins his mission. He heals sickness and disease among the people. He confronts God's enemies in the spiritual realm, the demons, and forcefully orders them to leave the people whom they torment. Jesus forgives the sins of those who humbly come to him. He proclaims the gospel, or good news, that:

> *Time's up! God's kingdom is here. Change your life and believe the*
> *Message. (Mark 1:15)*

The very heart of Jesus' Message is the good news of the coming of God's reign. God is coming back to dwell with his people. This is why Jesus is called Immanuel, which means "God with us."

But Jesus' message receives mixed responses. Some people believe, but most people simply watch him with amazement, never knowing quite what to make of him. The established religious leaders quickly become hostile toward him. Eventually this conflict escalates to the breaking point and the religious leaders conspire to have Jesus arrested and killed on a cross.

But this defeat is actually God's greatest victory. Jesus' death turns the tables on God's enemy and turns the world upside down. By willingly giving up his life as a sacrifice, Jesus takes onto himself God's judgment for our wrongdoing. He gives up his own life as a sacrifice for his people as Israel's true priest. He leads his people to a new Exodus, through death to a new life. In all of this Jesus shows himself to be the promised child of Abraham who reconciles humanity with God. It is through Jesus that Israel can finally fulfill its role, the purpose for which God called Abraham.

This account of Jesus is the focal point of the Bible's entire story. The key struggle with God's enemy, the desperate attempts to correct what has gone wrong at the very heart of things, comes to a head in the life of Jesus. He is the one and only hero of the story.

ACT V THE NEW PEOPLE OF GOD

If the key victory has already been secured, why is there an Act V? God wants the victory of Jesus to spread to all the nations of the world. Those who follow Jesus are being built into God's new temple, the place where God's Spirit lives. God is gathering these people from all around the world and forming them into his church. When this is complete, Jesus will return and the reign of God will become a reality throughout God's creation (1 Corinthians 15:24-25). The curse imposed during Act II will be removed (Revelation 22:3).

The task of bringing blessing to the peoples of the world has been given again to the descendants of Abraham. According to the New Testament, all those who belong to Christ are true children of Abraham (Galatians 3:29). Act V emphasizes the mission of Christ-followers: to proclaim and live out the liberating message of the good news of Christ's kingdom.

Act V moves through history to our own time, enveloping us in its drama. The Message of Christ and his kingdom has now come to us. The challenge of a decision now confronts us too. What will we do? How will we fit into this story?

The story of the Bible is the true account of the central conflict winding its way through the history of the world. Will we be a part of God's mission of re-creation — of restoring the world around us — and making the world (including ourselves) new?

What Now?

The most important thing you can do is to read these Scriptures carefully. God's Spirit uses them actively and powerfully to accomplish his purposes — in you and through you to impact the world.

The Bible is not necessarily an easy book to read. Some passages are difficult for everyone to understand. But if you stick with it, if you are committed to learning more about God and the story he's given us in the Bible, it will guide you, change you and keep you close to God.

THE DRAMA OF THE BIBLE

A Visual Chronology

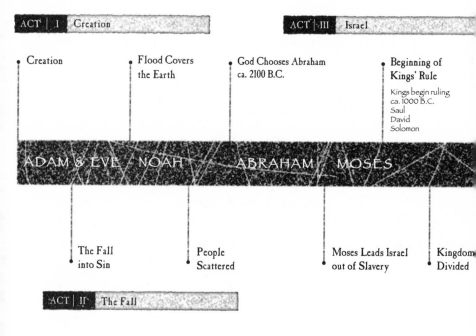

ACT | I   Creation

ACT | III   Israel

Creation

Flood Covers
the Earth

God Chooses Abraham
ca. 2100 B.C.

Beginning of
Kings' Rule

Kings begin ruling
ca. 1000 B.C.
Saul
David
Solomon

ADAM & EVE   NOAH   ABRAHAM   MOSES

The Fall
into Sin

People
Scattered

Moses Leads Israel
out of Slavery

Kingdom
Divided

ACT | II   The Fall

World Events

Pyramids built 2500s B.C.
Hinduism gains influence in India 1100s B.C.
Buddhism founded in India 500s B.C.
Alexander the Great begins rule 336 B.C.
China begins construction on The Great Wall 214 B.C.
Rise of the Roman Empire 28 B.C.

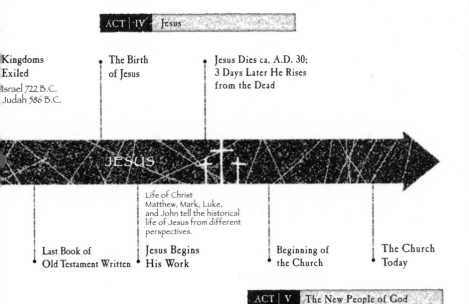

ACT | IV   Jesus

Kingdoms
Exiled
Israel 722 B.C.
Judah 586 B.C.

The Birth
of Jesus

Jesus Dies ca. A.D. 30;
3 Days Later He Rises
from the Dead

JESUS

Life of Christ
Matthew, Mark, Luke,
and John tell the historical
life of Jesus from different
perspectives.

Last Book of
Old Testament Written

Jesus Begins
His Work

Beginning of
the Church

The Church
Today

ACT | V   The New People of God

THE OLD TESTAMENT

THE BOOKS OF MOSES

STORIES AND SIGNPOSTS

An enormous authority and dignity have, through the centuries, developed around the first five books of the Bible, commonly known as The Books of Moses. Over the course of many centuries, they account for a truly astonishing amount of reading and writing, study and prayer, teaching and preaching.

God is the primary concern of these books. That accounts for the authority and the dignity. But it is not only God; we get included. That accounts for the widespread and intense human interest. We want to know what's going on. We want to know how we fit into things. We don't want to miss out.

The Books of Moses are made up mostly of stories and signposts. The stories show us God working with and speaking to men and women in a rich variety of circumstances. God is presented to us not in ideas and arguments but in events and actions that involve each of us personally. The signposts provide immediate and practical directions to guide us into behavior that is appropriate to our humanity and honoring to God.

The simplicity of the storytelling and signposting in these books makes what is written here as accessible to children as to adults. But the simplicity (as in so many simple things) is also profound, inviting us into a lifetime of growing participation in God's saving ways with us.

An image of human growth suggests a reason for the powerful pull of these stories and signposts on so many millions of men, women, and children to live as *God's* people. The sketch shows the five books as five stages of growth in which God creates first a cosmos and then a people for his glory.

Genesis is Conception. After establishing the basic elements by which God will do his work of creation and salvation and judgment in the midst of human sin and rebellion (chapters 1–11), God conceives a People to whom he will reveal himself as a God of salvation and through them, over time, to everyone on earth. God begins small, with one man: Abraham. He said to Abraham, "I am The Strong God, live entirely before me, live to the hilt! I'll make a covenant between us and I'll give you a huge family" (Genesis 17:1). The embryonic People of God grow in the womb. Gradually details and then more details become evident as the embryo takes shape: Sarah, Isaac, Rebekah, Jacob and Esau, Rachel, Joseph and his brothers. The pregnancy develops. Life is obviously developing in that womb, but there is also much that is not clear and visible. The background history is vague, the surrounding nations and customs veiled in a kind of mist. But the presence of life, God-conceived life, is kicking and robust.

Exodus is Birth and Infancy. The gestation of the People of God lasts a long time, but finally the birth pangs start. Egyptian slavery gives the first intimations of the contractions to come. When Moses arrives on the scene to preside over the birth itself, ten fierce plagues on Egypt accompany the contractions that bring the travail to completion: at the Red Sea the waters break, the People of God tumble out of the womb onto dry ground, and their life as a free People of God begins. Moses leads them crawling and toddling to Sinai. They are fed. God reveals himself to them at the mountain. They begin to get a sense of their Parent. They learn the language of freedom and salvation—a word here, a word there, the Ten Words (commandments) as a beginning, their basic vocabulary. The signposts begin to go up: do this; don't do that. But the largest part of their infant life is God, the living God. As they explore the deep and wide world of God, worship becomes their dominant and most important activity. An enormous amount of attention is given to training them in worship, building the structures for worship, mastering the procedures. They are learning how to give their full attention in obedience and adoration to God. As a result, "The Cloud [of God's presence] covered the Tent of Meeting, and the Glory of GOD filled The Dwelling. Moses couldn't enter the Tent of Meeting because the Cloud was upon it, and the Glory of GOD filled The Dwelling" (Exodus 40:34-35).

Leviticus is Schooling. As infancy develops into childhood, formal schooling takes place. There's a lot to know; they need some structure and arrangement to keep things straight: reading, writing, arithmetic. But for the People of God the basic curriculum has to do with God and their relationship with God. Leviticus is the *McGuffey's Reader* of the People of God. It is an almost totally audiovisual book, giving a picture and ritual in the sacrifices and feasts for the pivotal ways in which God's people keep alert and observant to the ways their relationship with God goes awry (sin) and the ways they are restored to forgiveness and innocence (salvation). Everyday life consists of endless and concrete detail, much of it having to do with our behavior before God and with one another, and so, of course, Leviticus necessarily consists also of endless detail which God took very seriously, saying, "Keep all my decrees and all my laws. Yes, *do* them. I am GOD" (Leviticus 19:37).

Numbers is Adolescence. The years of adolescence are critical to understanding who we are. We are advanced enough physically to be able, for the most part, to take care of ourselves. We are developed enough mentally, with some obvious limitations, to think for ourselves. We discover that we are not simply extensions of our parents; and we are not just mirror images of our culture. But who are we? Especially, who are we as a People of God? The People of God in Numbers are new at these emerging independent operations of behaving and thinking and so inevitably make a lot of mistakes. Rebellion is one of the more conspicuous mistakes. They test out their unique identity by rejecting the continuities with parents and culture. It's the easiest and cheapest way to "be myself" as we like to say. But it turns out that there isn't much to the "self" that is thus asserted. Maturity requires the integration, not the amputation, of what we have received through our conception and birth, our infancy and schooling. The People of God have an extraordinarily long adolescence in the wilderness — nearly forty years of it.

Deuteronomy is Adulthood. The mature life is a complex operation. Growing up is a long process. And growing up in God takes the longest time. During their forty years spent in the wilderness, the People of God developed from that full-term embryo brought to birth on the far shore of the Red Sea, are carried and led, nourished and protected under Moses to the place of God's Revelation at Sinai, taught and trained, disciplined and blessed. Now they are ready to live as free and obedient men and women in the new land, the Promised Land. They are ready for adulthood, ready to be as grown up inwardly as they are outwardly. They are ready to live as a free people, formed by God, as a holy people, transformed by God. They still have a long way to go (as do we all), but all the conditions for maturity are there. The book of Deuteronomy gathers up that entire process of becoming a People of God and turns it into a sermon and a song and a blessing. The strongest and key word in Deuteronomy is *love*. Moses told the people, "Love GOD, your God, with your whole heart: love him with all that's in you, love him with all you've got!" (Deuteronomy 6:5). Love is the most characteristic and comprehensive act of the human being. We are most ourselves when we love; we are most the People of God when we love. But love is not an abstract word defined out of a dictionary. In order to love maturely we have to live and absorb and enter into this world of salvation and freedom, find ourselves in the stories, become familiar with and follow the signposts, learn the life of worship, and realize our unique identity as the People of God who love.

The Books of Moses are foundational to the sixty-one books that follow in our Bibles. A foundation, though, is not a complete building but the anticipation of one. An elaborate moral infrastructure is provided here for what is yet to come. Each book that follows, in one way or another, picks up and develops some aspect of the messianic salvation involved in becoming the People of God, but it is always on this foundation. This foundation of stories and signposts has proved over and over to be solid and enduring.

A note on translating the name of God. In the original Hebrew text of the Old Testament, the generic name for divinity used by both Israel and its neighbors is translated God (or god). But the unique and distinctively personal name for God that was revealed to Moses at the burning bush (Exodus 3:13-14) I have translated as "GOD." The Jewish community early on substituted "LORD" for the unique name out of reverence (our lips are not worthy to speak The Name) and caution (lest we inadvertently blaspheme by saying God's name "in vain"). Most Christian translators continue in that practice.

GENESIS

God First and Last

First, God. God is the subject of life. God is foundational for living. If we don't have a sense of the primacy of God, we will never get it right, get life right, get *our* lives right. Not God at the margins; not God as an option; not God on the weekends. God at center and circumference; God first and last; God, God, God.

Genesis gets us off on the right foot. "First this: God" (Genesis 1:1). Genesis pulls us into a sense of reality that is God-shaped and God-filled. It gives us a vocabulary for speaking accurately and comprehensively about our lives, where we come from and where we are going, what we think and what we do, the people we live with and how to get along with them, the troubles we find ourselves in and the blessings that keep arriving.

Genesis uses words to make a foundation that is solid and true. Everything we think and do and feel is material in a building operation in which we are engaged all our life long. There is immense significance in everything that we do. Our speech and our actions and our prayers are all, every detail of them, involved in this vast building operation comprehensively known as the Kingdom of God. But we don't build the foundation. The foundation is given. The foundation is firmly in place.

Jesus concluded his most famous teaching by telling us that there are two ways to go about our lives — we can build on sand or we can build on rock. No matter how wonderfully we build, if we build on sand it will all fall to pieces like a house of cards. We build on what is already there, on the rock. Genesis is a verbal witness to that rock: God's creative acts, God's intervening and gracious judgments, God's call to a life of faith, God's making covenant with us.

God spoke: "Let us make human beings in our image, make them
    reflecting our nature
So they can be responsible for the fish in the sea,
    the birds in the air, the cattle,
And, yes, Earth itself,
    and every animal that moves on the face of Earth."
God created human beings;
    he created them godlike,
Reflecting God's nature.
    He created them male and female.
God blessed them:
    "Prosper! Reproduce! Fill Earth! Take charge!
Be responsible for fish in the sea and birds in the air,
    for every living thing that moves on the face of Earth." (Genesis 1:26-28)

But Genesis presents none of this to us as an abstract, bloodless "truth" or "principle." We are given a succession of stories with named people, people who loved and quarreled, believed and doubted, had children and married, experienced sin and grace. If we pay attention, we find that we ourselves are living variations on these very stories: Adam and Eve, Cain and Abel, Noah and his sons, Abraham and Sarah, Isaac and Rebekah, Jacob and Rachel, Joseph and his brothers. The stories show clearly that we are never outsiders or spectators to anything in "heaven and earth." God doesn't work impersonally from space; he works with us where we are, as he finds us. No matter what we do, whether good or bad, we continue to be part of everything that God is doing. Nobody can drop out — there's no place to drop out to. So we may as well get started and take our place in the story — at the beginning.

EXODUS

The Story of Salvation

The human race is in trouble. We've been in trouble for a long time. Enormous energies have been and continue to be expended by many, many men and women to get us out of the trouble we are in — to clean up the world's mess. The skill, the perseverance, the intelligence, the devotion of the people who put their shoulders to the wheel to pull us out of the muck — parents and teachers, healers and counselors, rulers and politicians, writers and pastors — are impressive.

At the center and core of this work is God. The most comprehensive term for what God is doing to get us out of the mess we are in is *salvation*. Salvation is God doing for us what we can't do for ourselves. Salvation is the biggest word in the vocabulary of the people of God. The Exodus is a powerful and dramatic and true story of God working salvation. He told his people, through Moses,

> *"I am GOD. I will bring you out from under the cruel hard labor of Egypt. I will rescue you from slavery. I will redeem you, intervening with great acts of judgment. I'll take you as my own people and I'll be God to you. You'll know that I am GOD, your God who brings you out from under the cruel hard labor of Egypt. I'll bring you into the land that I promised to give Abraham, Isaac, and Jacob and give it to you as your own country. I AM GOD." (Exodus 6:6-8)*

The story has generated an extraordinary progeny through the centuries as it has reproduced itself in song and poem, drama and novel, politics and social justice, repentance and conversion, worship and holy living. It continues to capture the imagination of men and women, especially men and women in trouble.

It is significant that God does not present us with salvation in the form of an abstract truth, or a precise definition or a catchy slogan, but as *story*. Exodus draws us into a story with plot and characters, which is to say, with design and personal relationships. Story is an invitation to participate, first through our imagination and then, if we will, by faith — with our total lives in response to God. This Exodus story continues to be a major means that God uses to draw men and women in trouble out of the mess of history into the kingdom of salvation.

About half the book (chapters 1–19 and 32–34) is a gripping narrative of an obscure and severely brutalized people who are saved from slavery into a life of freedom. The other half (chapters 20–31 and 35–40) is a meticulous, some think tedious, basic instruction and training in living the saved, free life. The story of salvation is not complete without both halves.

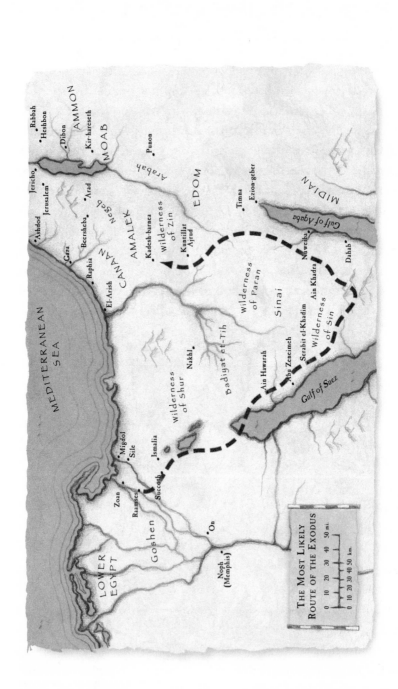

THE MOST LIKELY
ROUTE OF THE EXODUS

LEVITICUS

Holy as God Is Holy

One of the stubbornly enduring habits of the human race is to insist on domesticating God. We are determined to tame him. We figure out ways to harness God to our projects. We try to reduce God to a size that conveniently fits our plans and ambitions and tastes.

But our Scriptures are even more stubborn in telling us that we can't do it. God cannot be fit into our plans, we must fit into his. We can't use God — God is not a tool or appliance or credit card.

> *"Do what I tell you; live what I tell you. I am GOD.*
>
> *"Don't desecrate my holy name. I insist on being treated with holy reverence among the People of Israel. I am GOD who makes you holy and brought you out of Egypt to be your God. I am GOD." (Leviticus 22:31-33)*

"Holy" is the word that sets God apart and above our attempts to enlist him in our wish-fulfillment fantasies or our utopian schemes for making our mark in the world. Holy means that God is alive on God's terms, alive in a way that exceeds our experience and imagination. Holy refers to life burning with an intense purity that transforms everything it touches into itself.

Because the core of all living is God, and God is a holy God, we require much teaching and long training for living in response to God as he is and not as we want him to be. The book of Leviticus is a narrative pause in the story of our ancestors as they are on their way, saved out of Egypt, to settle in the land of Canaan. It is a kind of extended time-out of instruction, a detailed and meticulous preparation for living "holy" in a culture that doesn't have the faintest idea what "holy" is. The moment these people enter Canaan they will be picking their way through a lethal minefield of gods and goddesses that are designed to appeal to our god-fantasies: "Give us what we want when we want it on our own terms." What these god-fantasies in fact do is cripple or kill us. Leviticus is a start at the "much teaching and long training" that continues to be adapted and reworked in every country and culture where God is forming a saved people to live as he created them to live — holy as God is holy.

The first thing that strikes us as we read Leviticus in this light is that this holy God is actually present with us and virtually every detail of our lives is affected by the presence of this holy God; nothing in us, our relationships, or environment is left out. The second thing is that God provides a way (the sacrifices and feasts and Sabbaths) to bring everything in and about us into his holy presence, transformed in the fiery blaze of the holy. It is an awesome thing to come into his presence and we, like ancient Israel, stand in his presence at every moment (Psalm 139). Our Lord is not dwelling in a tent or house in our neighborhood. But he makes his habitation in us and among us as believers and says, "I am holy; you be holy" (1 Peter 1:16, citing Leviticus 11:44-45; 19:2; 20:7).

Once we realize this, the seemingly endless details and instructions of Leviticus become signposts of good news to us: God cares that much about the details of our lives, willing everything in and about us into the transformation that St. Paul later commended:

> So here's what I want you to do, God helping you: Take your everyday, ordinary life — your sleeping, eating, going-to-work, and walking-around life — and place it before God as an offering. Embracing what God does for you is the best thing you can do for him. Don't become so well-adjusted to your culture that you fit into it without even thinking.

Instead, fix your attention on God. You'll be changed from the inside out. Readily recognize what he wants from you, and quickly respond to it. Unlike the culture around you, always dragging you down to its level of immaturity, God brings the best out of you, develops well-formed maturity in you. (Romans 12:1-2)

NUMBERS

Growing Up

Becoming a truly human community is a long, complex, messy business. Simply growing up as a man or woman demands all the wisdom and patience and courage that we can muster. But growing up with others, parents and siblings and neighbors, to say nothing of odd strangers and mean enemies, immensely complicates the growing up.

The book of Numbers plunges us into the mess of growing up. The pages in this section of the biblical story give us a realistic feel for what is involved in being included in the people of God, which is to say, a human community that honors God, lives out love and justice in daily affairs, learns how to deal with sin in oneself and others, and follows God's commands into a future of blessing. And all this without illusions.

When the Cloud lifted above the Tent, the People of Israel marched out; and when the Cloud descended the people camped. The People of Israel marched at GOD's command and they camped at his command. As long as the Cloud was over The Dwelling, they camped. Even when the Cloud hovered over The Dwelling for many days, they honored GOD's command and wouldn't march. They stayed in camp, obedient to GOD's command, as long as the Cloud was over The Dwelling, but the moment GOD issued orders they marched. If the Cloud stayed only from sunset to daybreak and then lifted at daybreak, they marched. Night or day, it made no difference — when the Cloud lifted, they marched. It made no difference whether the Cloud hovered over The Dwelling for two days or a month or a year, as long as the Cloud was there, they were there. And when the Cloud went up, they got up and marched. They camped at

GOD's *command and they marched at* GOD's *command. They lived obe-diently by* GOD's *orders as delivered by Moses. (Numbers 9:17-23)*

Many of us fondle a romanticized spirituality in our imaginations. The "God's in his heaven/all's right with the world" sort of thing. When things don't go "right" we blame others or ourselves, muddle through as best we can, often with considerable crankiness, and wish that we had been born at a different time — "Bible times" maybe! — when living a holy life was so much easier. That's odd because the Bible, our primary text for showing us what it means to be a human being created by God and called to a life of obedient faith and sacrificial love, nowhere suggests that life is simple or even "natural." We need a lot of help.

We need organizational help. When people live together in community, jobs have to be assigned, leaders appointed, inventories kept. Counting and list-making and rosters are as much a part of being a community of God as prayer and instruction and justice. Accurate arithmetic is an aspect of becoming a people of God.

And we need relational help. The people who find themselves called and led and commanded by God find themselves in the company of men and women who sin a lot — quarrel, bicker, grumble, rebel, fornicate, steal — you name it, we do it. We need help in getting along with each other. Wise discipline is required in becoming a people of God.

It follows that counting and quarreling take up considerable space in the book of Numbers. Because they also continue to be unavoidable aspects of our becoming the people of God, this book is essential in training our imaginations to take in some of these less-than-romantic details by which we are formed into the people of God.

DEUTERONOMY

Live, Really Live

Deuteronomy is a sermon—actually a series of sermons. It is the longest sermon in the Bible and maybe the longest sermon ever. Deuteronomy presents Moses, standing on the Plains of Moab with all Israel assembled before him, preaching. It is his last sermon. When he completes it, he will leave his pulpit on the plains, climb a mountain, and die.

The setting is stirring and emotion-packed. Moses had entered the biblical story of salvation as a little baby born in Egypt under a death threat. Now, 120 years later, eyesight sharp as ever and walking with "a spring in his step," he preaches this immense sermon and dies, still brimming with words and life.

This sermon does what all sermons are intended to do: Take God's words, written and spoken in the past, take the human experience, ancestral and personal, of the listening congregation, then reproduce the words and experience as a single event right now, in this present moment. No word that God has spoken is a mere literary artifact to be studied; no human experience is dead history merely to be regretted or admired. The continuous and insistent Mosaic repetitions of "today" and "this day" throughout these sermons keep attentions taut and responsive. The complete range of human experience is brought to life and salvation by the full revelation of God: Live this! Now!

This commandment that I'm commanding you today isn't too much for you, it's not out of your reach. It's not on a high mountain — you don't have to get mountaineers to climb the peak and bring it down to your level and explain it before you can live it. And it's not across the

*ocean — you don't have to send sailors out to get it, bring it back, and
then explain it before you can live it. No. The word is right here and
now — as near as the tongue in your mouth, as near as the heart in your
chest. Just do it!*

Look at what I've done for you today: I've placed in front of you
    Life and Good
    Death and Evil.

*And I command you today: Love GOD, your God. Walk in his ways.
Keep his commandments, regulations, and rules so that you will live,
really live, live exuberantly, blessed by GOD, your God, in the land you
are about to enter and possess. (Deuteronomy 30:11-16)*

The Plains of Moab are the last stop on the forty-year journey from
Egyptian slavery to Promised Land freedom. The People of Israel have
experienced a lot as a congregation: deliverance, wanderings, rebel-
lions, wars, providence, worship, guidance. The People of Israel have
heard a lot from God: commandments, covenant conditions, sacrificial procedures. And now, poised at the River Jordan, ready to cross
over and possess the new land, Moses, preaching his great Plains of
Moab sermon, makes sure that they don't leave any of it behind, not
so much as one detail of their experience or God's revelation: He puts
their entire experience of salvation and providence into the present
tense (chapters 1–11); he puts the entire revelation of commandment
and covenant into the present tense (chapters 12–28); and then he
wraps it all up in a charge and a song and a blessing to launch them
into today's obedience and believing (chapters 29–34).

"Let's go."

THE HISTORY BOOKS

THE ORDINARY AND EXTRAORDINARY

The twelve biblical books stretching from Joshua to Esther are conventionally designated "the history books." But the word "history" doesn't tell the whole story, for this is history attentive to the conditions in which people encounter and experience God. The Hebrew people were intent on observing and participating in what happened in and around them because they believed that God was personally alive and active in the world, in their community, and in them.

GOD is our God! He brought up our ancestors from Egypt and from slave conditions. He did all those great signs while we watched. He has kept his eye on us all along the roads we've traveled and among the nations we've passed through. Just for us he drove out all the nations, Amorites and all, who lived in the land.

Count us in: We too are going to worship GOD. He's our God.
(Joshua 24:17-18)

Life could not be accounted for by something less than the life of God, no matter how impressive and mysterious their experience was, whether an eclipse of the sun, spots on the liver of a goat, or the hiss of steam from a fissure in the earth. God could not be reduced to astronomical, physiological, geological, or psychological phenomena; God was alive, always and everywhere working his will, challenging people with his call, evoking faith and obedience, shaping a worshiping community, showing his love and compassion, and working out judgments on sin. And none of this "in general" or "at large," but at particular times, in specific places, with named persons: history.

For biblical people, God is not an idea for philosophers to discuss or a force for priests to manipulate. God is not a part of creation that can be studied and observed and managed. God is person — a person to be worshiped or defied, believed or rejected, loved or hated, in time and place. That is why these books immerse us in dates and events, in persons and circumstances — in history. God meets us in the ordinary and extraordinary occurrences that make up the stuff of our daily lives. It never seemed to have occurred to our biblical ancestors that they could deal better with God by escaping from history, "getting away from it all" as we say. History is the medium in which God works salvation, just as paint and canvas is the medium in which Rembrandt made created works of art. We cannot get closer to God by distancing ourselves from the mess of history.

This deeply pervasive sense of history — the dignity of their place in history, the presence of God in history — accounts for the way in which the Hebrew people talked and wrote. They did not, as was the fashion in the ancient world, make up and embellish fanciful stories. Their writings did not entertain or explain; they revealed the ways of God with men and women and the world. They gave narrative shape to actual people and circumstances in their dealings with God, and in God's dealings with them.

Thank GOD! Call out his Name!
       Tell the whole world who he is and what he's done!
Sing to him! Play songs for him!
       Broadcast all his wonders!
Revel in his holy Name,
       GOD-seekers, be jubilant!
Study GOD and his strength,
       seek his presence day and night;
Remember all the wonders he performed,
       the miracles and judgments that came out of his mouth.
Seed of Israel his servant!
       Children of Jacob, his first choice!
He is our GOD, our God;
       wherever you go you come on his judgments and decisions.
He keeps his commitments across thousands
       of generations, the covenant he commanded,
The same one he made with Abraham,
       the very one he swore to Isaac;
He posted it in big block letters to Jacob,
       this eternal covenant with Israel:
"I give you the land of Canaan,
       this is your inheritance;
Even though you're not much to look at,
       a few straggling strangers."

They wandered from country to country,
       camped out in one kingdom after another;
But he didn't let anyone push them around,
       he stood up for them against bully-kings:
"Don't you dare touch my anointed ones,
       don't lay a hand on my prophets."

Sing to GOD, everyone and everything!
*   Get out his salvation news every day!*
Publish his glory among the godless nations,
*   his wonders to all races and religions.*
And why? Because GOD is great — well worth praising!
*   No god or goddess comes close in honor. (1 Chronicles 16:8-25)*

For the Hebrews there simply was no secular history. None. Everything that happened, happened in a world penetrated by God. Since they do not talk a lot about God in their storytelling, it is easy to forget that God is always the invisible and mostly silent presence in everything that is taking place. But if we forget for very long, we will understand neither what is written nor the way it is written. God is never absent from these narratives and never peripheral to them. As far as these writers were concerned, the only reason for paying attention to people and events was to stay alert to God.

This is a difficult mindset for us to acquire, for we are used to getting our history from so-called historians, scholars, and journalists for whom God is not involved or present in what they study and write. We are thoroughly trained by our schools, daily newspapers, and telecasts to read history solely in terms of politics and economics, human interest and environmental conditions. If we have a mind for it, we can go ahead and fit God in somewhere or other. These historical books — Joshua through Esther — are radically and refreshingly different. They pull us into a way of reading history that involves us and everyone around us in all the operations of God.

THE
TWELVE TRIBES

0   10   20   30 mi.

0 10 20 30 40   km.

THE DIVIDED KINGDOM
ISRAEL AND JUDAH

JOSHUA

The Gift of Land

Land. Land flowing with milk and honey. Promised land. Holy land. Canaan land. The land. Joshua, Moses' successor as leader of Israel, was poised at the River Jordan to enter and take possession of Canaan, an unremarkable stretch of territory sandwiched between massive and already ancient civilizations. It would have been unimaginable to anyone at the time that anything of significance could take place on that land. This narrow patch had never been significant economically or culturally, but only as a land bridge between the two great cultures and economies of Egypt and Mesopotamia. But it was about to become important in the religious consciousness of humankind. In significant ways, this land would come to dwarf everything that had gone on before and around it.

The People of Israel had been landless for nearly five hundred years. The "fathers" — Abraham, Isaac, Jacob and his twelve sons — had been nomads in the land of Canaan. That was followed by a long period of slavery in Egypt (over four hundred years!), a miraculous deliverance into freedom led by Moses, and then forty years of testing and training for living as a free people under God's guidance and blessing.

The company camped at the Jordan on the day that opens the book of Joshua had nearly half a millennium of slavery behind them. They were a dispossessed, ragtag crew — and only very recently set free. The transition from being landless slaves to landholding free men and women was huge. Joshua leads the transition, first in taking the land (chapters 1–12), then in distributing it among the twelve tribes (chapters 13–22), and concluding with a solemn covenant-witness (chapters 23–24) that bound the people to the gift of land and the worship of the God from whom they received it.

For most modern readers of Joshua, the toughest barrier to embracing this story as sacred is the military strategy of "holy war," what I have translated as the "holy curse"—killing everyone in the conquered cities and totally destroying all the plunder, both animals and goods. Massacre and destruction. "No survivors" is the recurrent refrain. We look back from our time in history and think, "How horrible." But if we were able to put ourselves back in the thirteenth century B.C., we might see it differently, for that Canaanite culture was a snake pit of child sacrifice and sacred prostitution, practices ruthlessly devoted to using the most innocent and vulnerable members of the community (babies and virgins) to manipulate God or gods for gain.

As the book of Joshua takes the story of salvation forward from the leadership and teaching of Moses, it continues to keep us grounded in places and connected to persons: place names, personal names—hundreds of them. What we often consider to be the subjects of religion—ideas, truths, prayers, promises, beliefs—are never permitted to have a life of their own apart from particular persons and actual places. Biblical religion has a low tolerance for "great ideas" or "sublime truths" or "inspirational thoughts" apart from the people and places in which they occur. God's great love and purposes for us are worked out in the messes, storms and sins, blue skies, daily work, and dreams of our common lives, working with us as we are and not as we should be. He said to Joshua (and us!), "Strength! Courage! Don't be timid; don't get discouraged. GOD, your God, is with you every step you take" (Joshua 1:9).

People who want God as an escape from reality, from the often hard conditions of this life, don't find this much to their liking. But to the man or woman wanting more reality, not less—this continuation of the salvation story—Joshua's fierce and devout determination to win land for his people and his extraordinary attention to getting all the tribes and their families name by name assigned to their own place, is good news indeed. Joshua lays a firm foundation for a life that is grounded.

JUDGES

His Best Work

Sex and violence, rape and massacre, brutality and deceit do not seem to be congenial materials for use in developing a story of salvation. Given the Bible's subject matter — God and salvation, living well and loving deeply — we quite naturally expect to find in its pages leaders for us who are good, noble, honorable men and women showing us the way. So it is always something of a shock to enter the pages of the book of Judges and find ourselves immersed in nearly unrelieved mayhem. Over and over we read, "The People of Israel did evil in GOD's sight" (Judges 2:11; 3:12; 4:1; 6:1; 10:6; 13:1).

It might not gravel our sensibilities so much if these flawed and reprobate leaders were held up as negative moral examples, with lurid, hellfire descriptions of the punishing consequences of living such bad lives. But the story is not told quite that way. There is a kind of matter-of-fact indifference in the tone of the narration, almost as if God is saying, "Well, if this is all you're going to give me to work with, I'll use *these* men and women, just as they are, and get on with working out the story of salvation." These people are even given a measure of dignity as they find their place in the story; they are most certainly not employed for the sake of vilification or lampoon.

God, it turns out, does not require good people in order to do good work. He can and does work with us in whatever moral and spiritual condition he finds us. God, we are learning, does some of his best work using the most unlikely people. If God found a way to significantly include these leaders ("judges") in what we know is on its way to becoming a glorious conclusion, he can certainly use us along with our sometimes impossible friends and neighbors.

Twice in Judges (17:6 and 21:25) there is the telling refrain: "at that time there was no king in Israel. People did whatever they felt like doing." But we readers know that there *was* a king in Israel: *God* was king. And so, while the lack of an earthly king accounts for the moral and political anarchy, the presence of the sovereign God, however obscurely realized, means that the reality of the kingdom is never in doubt.

Ruth

The Great-Grandmother of David

As we read the broad, comprehensive biblical story of God at work in the world, most of us are entirely impressed: God speaking creation into being, God laying the foundations of the life of faith through great and definitive fathers and mothers, God saving a people out of a brutal slave existence and then forming them into lives of free and obedient love, God raising up leaders who direct and guide through the tangle of difficulties always involved in living joyfully and responsively before God.

Very impressive. So impressive, in fact, that many of us, while remaining impressed, feel left out. Our unimpressive, very ordinary lives make us feel like outsiders to such a star-studded cast. We disqualify ourselves. Guilt or willfulness or accident makes a loophole and we assume that what is true for everyone else is not true for us. We conclude that we are, somehow, "just not religious" and thus unfit to participate in the big story.

And then we turn a page and come on this small story of two widows and a farmer in their out-of-the-way village.

The outsider Ruth was not born into the faith and felt no natural part of it — like many of us. But she came to find herself gathered into the story and given a quiet and obscure part that proved critical to the way everything turned out.

Scripture is a vast tapestry of God's creating, saving, and blessing ways in this world. The great names in the plot that climaxes at Sinai (Abraham, Isaac, Jacob, Joseph, Moses) and the great names in the sequel (Joshua, Samuel, David, Solomon) can be intimidating to ordinary, random individuals: "Surely there is no way that I can have any significant part on such a stage." But the story of the widowed, impoverished, alien Ruth is proof to the contrary. She is the inconsequential outsider whose life turns out to be essential for telling the complete story of God's ways among us. The unassuming ending carries the punch line: Boaz married Ruth, she had a son Obed, "Obed was the father of Jesse, and Jesse the father of David" (Ruth 4:17).

David! In its artful telling of this "outsider" widow, uprooted and obscure, who turns out to be the great-grandmother of David and the ancestor of Jesus, the book of Ruth makes it possible for each of us to understand ourselves, however ordinary or "out of it," as irreplaceable in the full telling of God's story. We count — every last one of us — and what we do counts.

1 & 2 Samuel

The Millennial Midpoint

Four lives dominate the two-volume narrative, First and Second Samuel: Hannah, Samuel, Saul, and David. Chronologically, the stories are clustered around the year 1000 B.C., the millennial midpoint between the call of Abraham, the father of Israel, nearly a thousand years earlier (about 1800 B.C.) and the birth of Jesus, the Christ, a thousand years later.

These four lives become seminal for us at the moment we realize that our ego-bound experience is too small a context in which to understand and experience what it means to believe in God and follow his ways. For these are large lives — large because they live in the largeness of God. Not one of them can be accounted for in terms of cultural conditions or psychological dynamics; God is the country in which they live.

Most of us need to be reminded that these stories are not exemplary in the sense that we stand back and admire them, like statues in a gallery, knowing all the while that we will never be able to live either that gloriously or tragically ourselves. Rather they are immersions into the actual business of living itself: this is what it means to be human. Reading and praying our way through these pages, we get it; gradually but most emphatically we recognize that what it means to be a woman, a man, mostly has to do with God. These four stories do not show us how we should live but how in fact we do live, authenticating the reality of our daily experience as the stuff that God uses to work out his purposes of salvation in us and in the world.

The stories do not do this by talking about God, for there is surprisingly little explicit God talk here — whole pages sometimes without the name of God appearing. But as the narrative develops we realize that God is the commanding and accompanying presence that provides both plot and texture to every sentence. This cluster of interlocking stories trains us in perceptions of ourselves, our sheer and irreducible humanity, that cannot be reduced to personal feelings or ideas or circumstances. If we want a life other than mere biology, we must deal with God. There is no alternate way.

One of many welcome consequences in learning to "read" our lives in the lives of Hannah, Samuel, Saul, and David is a sense of affirmation and freedom: we don't have to fit into prefabricated moral or mental or religious boxes before we are admitted into the company of God — we are taken seriously just as we are and given a place in his story, for it is, after all, his story; none of us is the leading character in the story of our life. Hannah and David understood this, as evidenced by their prayers.

Hannah prayed:

> *Nothing and no one is holy like* God,
> *no rock mountain like our God.*
> *Don't dare talk pretentiously —*
> *not a word of boasting, ever!*
> *For* God *knows what's going on.*
> *He takes the measure of everything that happens. . . .*

> God *brings death and* God *brings life,*
> *brings down to the grave and raises up.*
> God *brings poverty and* God *brings wealth;*
> *he lowers, he also lifts up. . . .*
> *For the very structures of the earth are* God's;
> *he has laid out his operations on a firm foundation.*
> *He protectively cares for his faithful friends, step by step,*
> *but leaves the wicked to stumble in the dark.*
> *No one makes it in this life by sheer muscle!* (1 Samuel 2:2, 6-9)

David prayed,

> GOD is bedrock under my feet,
> > the castle in which I live,
> > my rescuing knight.
> My God — the high crag
> > where I run for dear life,
> > hiding behind the boulders,
> > safe in the granite hideout;
> My mountaintop refuge,
> > he saves me from ruthless men.

> I sing to GOD the Praise-Lofty,
> > and find myself safe and saved. . . .

> GOD made my life complete
> > when I placed all the pieces before him. (2 Samuel 22:1-4,21)

Samuel clearly understood it, too, and tried to enlighten Saul. He said,

> Do you think all GOD wants are sacrifices —
> > empty rituals just for show?
> He wants you to listen to him!
> Plain listening is the thing,
> > not staging a lavish religious production.
> Not doing what GOD tells you
> > is far worse than fooling around in the occult.
> Getting self-important around GOD
> > is far worse than making deals with your dead ancestors.

Because you said No to God's command,
    he says No to your kingship. (1 Samuel 15:22-23)

The biblical way is not so much to present us with a moral code and tell us "Live up to this"; nor is it to set out a system of doctrine and say, "Think like this and you will live well." The biblical way is to tell a story and invite us, "Live into this. This is what it looks like to be human; this is what is involved in entering and maturing as human beings." We do violence to the biblical revelation when we "use" it for what we can get out of it or what we think will provide color and spice to our otherwise bland lives. That results in a kind of "boutique spirituality" — God as decoration, God as enhancement. The Samuel narrative will not allow that. In the reading, as we submit our lives to what we read, we find that we are not being led to see God in our stories but to see our stories in God's. God is the larger context and plot in which our stories find themselves.

Such reading will necessarily be a prayerful reading — a God-listening, God-answering reading. The story, after all, is framed by prayer: Hannah's prayer at the beginning (1 Samuel 2), and David's near the end (2 Samuel 22–23).

1 & 2 KINGS

A Wild and Extravagant Notion

Sovereignty, *God's* sovereignty, is one of the most difficult things for people of faith to live out in everyday routines. But we have no choice: God is Sovereign. God rules. Not only in our personal affairs but in the cosmos. Not only in our times and places of worship but in office buildings, political affairs, factories, universities, hospitals — yes, even behind the scenes in saloons and rock concerts. It's a wild and extravagant notion, to be sure. But nothing in our Scriptures is attested to more frequently or emphatically.

Yet not much in our daily experience confirms it. Impersonal forces and arrogant egos compete for the last word in power. Most of us are knocked around much of the time by forces and wills that give no hint of God. Still, generation after generation, men and women of sound mind continue to give sober witness to God's sovereign rule. One of the enduring titles given to Jesus is "King."

So how do we manage to live believingly and obediently in and under this revealed sovereignty in a world that is mostly either ignorant or defiant of it?

Worship shaped by an obedient reading of Scripture is basic. We submit to having our imaginations and behaviors conditioned by the reality of God rather than by what is handed out in school curricula and media reporting. In the course of this worshipful listening, the books of Kings turn out to provide essential data on what we can expect as we live under God's sovereign rule.

The story of our ancestors, the Hebrew kings, began in the books of Samuel. This story makes it clear that it was not God's idea that the Hebrews have a king, but since they insisted, he let them have their way. But God never abdicated his sovereignty to any of the Hebrew

kings; the idea was that they would represent *his* sovereignty, not that
he would delegate his sovereignty to them.

But it never worked very well. After five hundred years and something over forty kings, there was not much to show for it. Even the
bright spots — David and Hezekiah and Josiah — were not *very* bright.
Human beings, no matter how well intentioned or gifted, don't seem
to be able to represent God's rule anywhere close to satisfactory. The
books of Kings, in that light, are a relentless exposition of failure — a
relentless five-hundred-year documentation proving that the Hebrew
demand of God to "have a king" was about the worst thing they could
have asked for.

But through the centuries, readers of this text have commonly realized something else: In the midst of the incredible mess these kings are
making of God's purposes, God continues to work his purposes and
uses them in the work — doesn't discard them, doesn't detour around
them; he uses them. They are part of his sovereign rule, whether they
want to be or not, whether they know it or not. Hezekiah had at least
some idea. In his prayer for deliverance from Assyria, he said,

> GOD, God of Israel, seated
> >   in majesty on the cherubim-throne.
> You are the one and only God,
> >   sovereign over all kingdoms on earth,
> Maker of heaven,
> >   maker of earth.
> Open your ears, GOD, and listen,
> >   open your eyes and look. . . .
> Make all the kingdoms on earth know
> >   that you are GOD, the one and only God. (2 Kings 19:15-16,19)

God's purposes *are* worked out in confrontation and revelation, in judgment and salvation, but they are worked out. Addressing the Assyrians, he said, "Did it never occur to you that I'm behind all this? Long, long ago I drew up the plans, and now I've gone into action" (2 Kings 19:25). God's rule is not imposed in the sense that he forces each man and woman into absolute conformity to justice and truth and righteousness. The rule is worked from within, much of the time invisible and unnoticed, but always patiently and resolutely *there*. The books of Kings provide a premier witness to the sovereignty of God carried out among some of the most unlikely and uncooperative people who have ever lived.

The benefit of reading these books is enormous. To begin with, our understanding and experience of God's sovereignty develops counter to all power-based and piety-based assumptions regarding God's effective rule. We quit spinning our wheels on utopian projects and dreams. Following that, we begin to realize that if God's sovereignty is never canceled out by the so deeply sin-flawed leaders ("kings") in both our culture and our church, we can quite cheerfully exult in God's sovereignty as it is being exercised (though often silently and hiddenly) in all the circumstantial details of the actual present.

1 & 2 Chronicles

The Place of Worship

There is always more than one way to tell a story. The story of Israel's kings is first narrated in the books of Samuel and Kings. Here is another telling of the same story, a hundred or so years later, by another voice and from another perspective: Chronicles. Some of the earlier narrative is omitted and there are substantial additions but it is recognizably the same story. But Israel's fortunes have changed considerably since the earlier authoritative writing (Genesis through Kings); God's people are in danger of losing touch with what made them God's people in the first place. In retrospect, from the low point in their history in which they now find themselves, it looks very much like a succession of world powers; Assyria and Egypt, Babylon and Persia, have been calling all the shots. The People of Israel are swamped by alien influences; they are also, it seems, mired in internal religious pettiness; will they be obliterated?

A new writer (it may have been Ezra) took it in hand to tell the old and by now familiar story but with a new slant. His task was to recover and restore Israel's confidence and obedience as God's people. Remarkably — and improbably, considering the political and cultural conditions of the time — this writer insisted, with very little "hometown" support, on the core identity of Israel as a worshiping people in the Davidic tradition. And he did it all by writing the two books of Chronicles. Israel did not finally disappear into the ancient Near East melting pot of violence and sex and religion.

Names launch this story, hundreds and hundreds of names, lists of names, page after page of names, *personal* names. There is no true storytelling without names, and this immersion in names calls attention to the individual, the unique, the personal, which is inherent in all spirituality. Name lists (genealogies) occur in other places in Scripture (Genesis, Numbers, Matthew, Luke) but none as extravagantly copious as here. Holy history is not constructed from impersonal forces or abstract ideas; it is woven from names — persons, each one unique. Chronicles erects a solid defense against depersonalized religion.

And Chronicles provides a witness to the essential and primary place of accurate worship in human life. The narrative backbone of Chronicles is worship — the place of worship (the Jerusalem Temple), the ministers of worship (the priests and Levites), the musical components of worship (both vocal and instrumental), and the authoritative role of King David, the master of worship, who maintains faithfulness and integrity in worship. Shortly before his death, doing as he had done throughout his life and in response to the generosity of the people,

David blessed GOD in full view of the entire congregation:

Blessed are you, GOD of Israel, our father
    from of old and forever.
To you, O GOD, belong the greatness and the might,
    the glory, the victory, the majesty, the splendor;
Yes! Everything in heaven, everything on earth;
    the kingdom all yours! You've raised yourself high over all.
Riches and glory come from you,
    you're ruler over all;
You hold strength and power in the palm of your hand
    to build up and strengthen all.
And here we are, O God, our God, giving thanks to you,
    praising your splendid Name. (1 Chronicles 29:10-13)

Some time later, after David's son Solomon finished building The
Temple,

He knelt in full view of the whole congregation, stretched his hands to
heaven, and prayed:

> GOD, O God of Israel, there is no God like you in the skies above
> or on the earth below, who unswervingly keeps covenant with his ser-
> vants and unfailingly loves them while they sincerely live in obedience to
> your way. You kept your word to David my father, your promise. You
> did exactly what you promised — every detail. The proof is before us
> today!. . .
> Can it be that God will actually move into our neighborhood? Why
> the cosmos itself isn't large enough to give you breathing room, let alone
> this Temple I've built. Even so, I'm bold to ask: Pay attention to these
> my prayers, both intercessory and personal, O GOD, my God. Listen to
> my prayers, energetic and devout, that I'm setting before you right now.
> Keep your eyes open to this Temple day and night, this place you prom-
> ised to dignify with your Name. And listen to the prayers that I pray in
> this place. And listen to your people Israel when they pray at this place.
> (2 Chronicles 6:13-15,18-21)

In the way this story of Israel's past is told, nothing takes precedence over worship in nurturing and protecting our identity as a
people of God — not politics, not economics, not family life, not art.
And nothing in the preparation for and conduct of worship is too
small to be left to whim or chance — nothing in architecture, person-
nel, music, or theology.

Earlier threats to Israel's identity and survival as a people of
God frequently came in the form of hostile outsiders — Egyptians,

Canaanites, Philistines, Amalekites, and others; but in this assessment of what matters, right and faithful worship turns out to be what counts most of all. The people of God are not primarily a political entity or a military force or an economic power; they are a holy congregation diligent in worship. To lose touch with the Davidic (and Moses-based) life of worship is to disintegrate as a holy people. To be seduced by the popular pagan worship of the surrounding culture is to be obliterated as a holy people.

Not many readers of this text will find their names in the lists of names in this book. Few worshiping congregations will recognize architectural continuities between The Temple and their local church sanctuaries. Not many communities have access to a pool of Levites from which to recruit choirs and appoint leaders of worship. So, what's left?

Well, worship is left — and names. Accurate worship, defined and fed by the God who reveals himself in Jesus Christ. And personal names that add up to a people of God, a holy congregation. Christians have characteristically read and prayed themselves into Chronicles in order to stay alert to the irreducibly personal in all matters of faith and practice, and to maintain a critical awareness that the worship of God is the indispensable foundation for living whole and redeemed lives.

EZRA

Worship and Text

History had not treated the People of Israel well and they were in decline. A superpower military machine, Babylon, had battered them and then, leaving their city and temple a mound of rubble, hauled them off into exile. Now, 128 years later, a few Jews back in Jerusalem had been trying to put the pieces back together decade after weary decade. But it was not going well at all. They were hanging on by their fingernails. And then Ezra arrived.

This is an extreme case of a familiar story, repeated with variations in most centuries and in most places in the world. Men and women who find their basic identity in God, as God reveals himself in Israel and Messiah, don't find an easy time of it. They never have. They never will. Their identity is under constant challenge and threat — sometimes by hostile assault, at other times by subtle and smiling seductions. Whether by assault or seduction, the People of God have come perilously close to obliteration several times. We are never out of danger.

Because of Ezra, Israel made it through. God didn't leave Ezra to do this single-handedly; he gave him substantial and critical help in the rescue operation in the person of Nehemiah, whose work providentially converged with his. (Important details of the Ezra story are in the memoirs of Nehemiah, the book that follows this one.) The People-of-God identity was recovered and preserved. Ezra used Worship and Text to do it. Ezra engaged them in the worship of God, the most all-absorbing, comprehensive act in which men and women can engage. This is how our God-formed identities become most deeply embedded in us. A spokesman for the people encouraged Ezra: "Let's make a covenant right now with our God. . . . It's what The Revelation says, so let's do it. Now get up, Ezra. Take charge — we're behind you. Don't back down" (Ezra 10:3-4). And Ezra led them into an obedient listening to the text of Scripture. Listening and following God's revelation are the primary ways in which we keep attentively obedient to the living presence of God among us.

Ezra made his mark: Worship and Text continue to be foundational for recovering and maintaining identity as the People of God.

NEHEMIAH

Stones and Mortar

Separating life into distinct categories of "sacred" and "secular" damages, sometimes irreparably, any attempt to live a whole and satisfying life, a coherent life with meaning and purpose, a life lived to the glory of God. Nevertheless, the practice is widespread. But where did all these people come up with the habit of separating themselves and the world around them into these two camps? It surely wasn't from the Bible. The Holy Scriptures, from beginning to end, strenuously resist such a separation.

The damage to life is most obvious when the separation is applied to daily work. It is common for us to refer to the work of pastors, priests, and missionaries as "sacred," and that of lawyers, farmers, and engineers as "secular." It is also wrong. Work, by its very nature, is holy. The biblical story is dominated by people who have jobs in gardening, shepherding, the military, politics, carpentry, tent making, homemaking, fishing, and more.

Nehemiah is one of these. He started out as a government worker in the employ of a foreign king. Then he became — and this is the work he tells us of in these memoirs — a building contractor, called in to rebuild the walls of Jerusalem. His coworker Ezra was a scholar and teacher, working with the Scriptures. Nehemiah worked with stones and mortar. The stories of the two men are interwoven in a seamless fabric of vocational holiness. In fact, Nehemiah 6:16 says even "the surrounding nations . . . knew that God was behind this work." Neither job was more or less important or holy than the other. Nehemiah needed Ezra; Ezra needed Nehemiah. God's people needed the work of both of them. We still do.

ESTHER

The Final and Definitive Word

It seems odd that the awareness of God, or even of the people of God, brings out the worst in some people. God, the source of all goodness and blessing and joy, at times becomes the occasion for nearly unimaginable acts of cruelty, atrocity, and evil.

There is a long history of killing men and women simply because they are perceived as reminders or representatives of the living God, as if killing people who worship God gets rid of God himself. We've recently completed a century marked by an extraordinary frenzy of such "god" killings. To no one's surprise, God is still alive and present.

The book of Esther opens a window on this world of violence directed, whether openly or covertly, against God and God's people. The perspective it provides transcends the occasion that provoked it, a nasty scheme to massacre all the exiled Jews who lived in the vast expanse of fifth-century B.C. Persia. Three characters shape the plot. Mordecai, identified simply as "the Jew," anchors the story. He is solid, faithful, sane, godly. His goodness is more than matched by the evil and arrogant vanity of Haman, who masterminds the planned massacre. Mordecai's young, orphaned, and ravishing cousin, Esther, whom he has raised, emerges from the shadows of the royal harem to take on the title role.

It turns out that no God-representing men and women get killed in this story — in a dramatic turnaround, the plot fails.

King Xerxes said to Queen Esther and Mordecai the Jew: "I've given Haman's estate to Esther and he's been hanged on the gallows because he

attacked the Jews. So go ahead now and write whatever you decide on
behalf of the Jews." . . .

The king's order authorized the Jews in every city to arm and
defend themselves to the death, killing anyone who threatened them or
their women and children.

. . . Not one man was able to stand up against them — fear made
cowards of them all. (Esther 8:7-8,11; 9:2)

But millions before and after Esther have been and, no doubt, will
continue to be killed. There is hardly a culture or century that doesn't
eventually find a Haman determined to rid the world of evidence and
reminders of God. Meanwhile, Esther continues to speak the final
and definitive word: You can't eliminate God's people. No matter how
many of them you kill, you can't get rid of the communities of God-
honoring, God-serving, God-worshiping people scattered all over the
earth. This is still the final and definitive word.

The Wisdom Books

Human Experience

There is a distinctive strain of writing in the Bible that more or less specializes in dealing with human experience — as is. *This* is what is involved in being human, and don't you forget it. "Wisdom" is the common designation given to this aspect of biblical witness and writing.

The word in this context refers more to a kind of attitude, a distinctive stance, than to any particular ideas or doctrines or counsel. As such, Wisdom is wide-ranging, collecting under its umbrella diverse and unlikely fellow travelers. What keeps the feet of these faith-travelers on common ground is Wisdom's unrelenting insistence that nothing in human experience can be omitted or slighted if we decide to take God seriously and respond to him believingly.

God and God's ways provide the comprehensive plot and sovereign action in the Holy Scriptures, but human beings — every last man and woman of us, including every last detail involved in our daily living — are invited and honored participants in all of it. There are no spectator seats provided for the drama of salvation. There is no "bench" for incompetent players.

It is fairly common among people who get interested in religion or God to get proportionately *dis*interested in their jobs and families, their communities and their colleagues — the more of God, the less of the human. But that is not the way God intends it. Wisdom counters this tendency by giving witness to the precious nature of human experience in all its forms, whether or not it feels or appears "spiritual."

Job, Psalms, Proverbs, Ecclesiastes, and the Song of Songs serve as our primary witnesses to biblical Wisdom. It is not as if wisdom is confined to these books, for its influence is pervasive throughout Scripture. But in these books human experience as the arena in which God is present and working is placed front and center.

The comprehensiveness of these five witnesses becomes evident when we set Psalms at the center, and then crisscross that center with the other four arranged as two sets of polarities: first Job and Proverbs, and then Ecclesiastes and the Song of Songs.

Psalms is a magnetic center, pulling every scrap and dimension of human experience into the presence of God. The Psalms are indiscriminate in their subject matter — complaint ("I'm fading away to nothing") and thanks ("applaud GOD!"), doubt ("Where is the love you're so famous for, Lord?") and anger ("O, God, give them their just deserts!"), outcries of pain ("Not a day goes by but somebody beats me up") and outbursts of joy ("Shout God-songs at the top of your lungs!"), quiet reflection ("I ponder every morsel of wisdom from you") and boisterous worship ("Bravo, GOD, bravo!"). If it's *human*, it qualifies. Any human experience, feeling, or thought can be prayed. Eventually it all *must* be prayed if it is to retain — or recover — its essential humanity. The totality of God's concern with the totality of our humanity is then elaborated by means of the two polarities.

The Job-Proverbs polarity sets the crisis experience of extreme suffering opposite the routine experience of getting along as best we can in the ordinary affairs of work and family, money and sex, the use of language and the expression of emotions.

"Why does God bother giving light to the miserable,
*   why bother keeping bitter people alive,*
Those who want in the worst way to die, and can't,
*   who can't imagine anything better than death,*
Who count the day of their death and burial
*   the happiest day of their life?*
What's the point of life when it doesn't make sense,
*   when God blocks all the roads to meaning?" (Job 3:20-23)*

These are the wise sayings of Solomon, . . .
Written down so we'll know how to live well and right,
*   to understand what life means and where it's going;*
A manual for living,
*   for learning what's right and just and fair;*
To teach the inexperienced the ropes
*   and give our young people a grasp on reality.*
There's something here also for seasoned men and women,
*   still a thing or two for the experienced to learn —*
Fresh wisdom to probe and penetrate,
*   the rhymes and reasons of wise men and women. (Proverbs 1:1-6)*

The life of faith has to do with extraordinary experience; the life of faith has to do with ordinary experience. Neither cancels out the other; neither takes precedence over the other. As Job rages in pain and protest, we find that the worst that can happen to us has been staked out as God's territory. As the pithy Proverbs sharpen our observations and insights regarding what is going on all around us, we realize that all this unobtrusive, undramatic dailiness is also God's country.

The Song-Ecclesiastes polarity sets the ecstatic experience of love in tension with the boredom of the same old round.

Kiss me — full on the mouth!
> *Yes! For your love is better than wine,*
> *headier than your aromatic oils. . . .*

Take me away with you! . . .
We'll celebrate, we'll sing,
> *we'll make great music.*
Yes! For your love is better than vintage wine. (Song of Songs 1:2-4)

Everything's boring, utterly boring —
> *no one can find any meaning in it.*
Boring to the eye,
> *boring to the ear.*
What was will be again,
> *what happened will happen again. (Ecclesiastes 1:8-9)*

The life of faith has to do with the glories of discovering far more in life than we ever dreamed of; the life of faith has to do with doggedly putting one flat foot in front of the other, wondering what the point of it all is. Neither cancels out the other; neither takes precedence over the other. As we sing and pray the lyrics of the Song of Songs, we become convinced that God blesses the best that human experience is capable of; as we ponder the sardonic verses of Ecclesiastes, we recognize the limits inherent in all human experience, appreciate it for what it is, but learn not to confuse it with God.

In such ways, these Wisdom writers keep us honest with and attentive to the entire range of human experience that God the Spirit uses to fashion a life of holy salvation in each of us.

JOB

Entering the Mystery

Job suffered. His name is synonymous with suffering. He asked, "Why?" He asked, "Why me?" And he put his questions to God. He asked his questions persistently, passionately, and eloquently. He refused to take silence for an answer. He refused to take clichés for an answer. He refused to let God off the hook.

Job did not take his sufferings quietly or piously. He disdained going for a second opinion to outside physicians or philosophers. Job took his stand before *God*, and there he protested his suffering, protested mightily.

> *"All I want is an answer to one prayer,*
> *a last request to be honored:*
> *Let God step on me — squash me like a bug,*
> *and be done with me for good.*
> *I'd at least have the satisfaction*
> *of not having blasphemed the Holy God,*
> *before being pressed past the limits.*
> *Where's the strength to keep my hopes up?*
> *What future do I have to keep me going?*
> *Do you think I have nerves of steel?*
> *Do you think I'm made of iron?*
> *Do you think I can pull myself up by my bootstraps?*
> *Why, I don't even have any boots!"(Job 6:8-13)*

It is not only because Job suffered that he is important to us. It is because he suffered in the same ways that *we* suffer — in the vital areas of family, personal health, and material things. Job is also important to us because he searchingly questioned and boldly protested his suffering. Indeed, he went "to the top" with his questions.

It is not suffering as such that troubles us. It is undeserved suffering.

Almost all of us in our years of growing up have the experience of disobeying our parents and getting punished for it. When that discipline was connected with wrongdoing, it had a certain sense of justice to it: *When we do wrong, we get punished.*

One of the surprises as we get older, however, is that we come to see that there is no real correlation between the amount of wrong we commit and the amount of pain we experience. An even larger surprise is that very often there is something quite the opposite: we do right and get knocked down. We do the best we are capable of doing, and just as we are reaching out to receive our reward we are hit from the blind side and sent reeling.

This is the suffering that first bewilders and then outrages us. This is the kind of suffering that bewildered and outraged Job, for Job was doing everything right when suddenly everything went wrong. And it is this kind of suffering to which Job gives voice when he protests to God.

Job gives voice to his sufferings so well, so accurately and honestly, that anyone who has ever suffered — which includes every last one of us — can recognize his or her personal pain in the voice of Job. Job says boldly what some of us are too timid to say. He makes poetry out of what in many of us is only a tangle of confused whimpers. He shouts out to God what a lot of us mutter behind our sleeves. He refuses to accept the role of a defeated victim.

I know that God lives — the One who gives me back my life —
    and eventually he'll take his stand on earth.
And I'll see him — even though I get skinned alive! —
    see God myself, with my very own eyes.
    Oh, how I long for that day! (Job 19:25-27)

It is also important to note what Job does *not* do, lest we expect something from him that he does not intend. Job does not curse God as his wife suggests he should do, getting rid of the problem by getting rid of God. But neither does Job *explain* suffering. He does not instruct us in how to live so that we can avoid suffering. Suffering is a mystery, and Job comes to respect the mystery.

"He [God] knows where I am and what I've done.
    He can cross-examine me all he wants, and I'll pass the test
        with honors.
I've followed him closely, my feet in his footprints,
    not once swerving from his way.
I've obeyed every word he's spoken
    and not just obeyed his advice — I've treasured it.

But he is singular and sovereign. Who can argue with him?
    He does what he wants, when he wants to.
He'll complete in detail what he's decided about me,
    and whatever else he determines to do.
Is it any wonder that I dread meeting him?
    Whenever I think about it, I get scared all over again." (Job 23:10-15)

In the course of facing, questioning, and respecting suffering, Job finds himself in an even larger mystery — the mystery of God. Perhaps the greatest mystery in suffering is how it can bring a person into the presence of God in a state of worship, full of wonder, love, and praise. Suffering does not inevitably do that, but it does it far more often than we would expect. It certainly did that for Job. Even in his answer to his wife he speaks the language of an uncharted irony, a dark and difficult kind of truth: "We take the good days from God — why not also the bad days?"

But there is more to the book of Job than Job. There are Job's friends. The moment we find ourselves in trouble of any kind — sick in the hospital, bereaved by a friend's death, dismissed from a job or relationship, depressed or bewildered — people start showing up telling us exactly what is wrong with us and what we must do to get better. Sufferers attract fixers the way roadkills attract vultures. At first we are impressed that they bother with us and amazed at their facility with answers. They know so much! How did they get to be such experts in living?

More often than not, these people use the Word of God frequently and loosely. They are full of spiritual diagnosis and prescription. It all sounds so hopeful. But then we begin to wonder, "Why is it that for all their apparent compassion we feel worse instead of better after they've said their piece?"

The book of Job is not only a witness to the dignity of suffering and God's presence in our suffering but is also our primary biblical protest against religion that has been reduced to explanations or "answers." Many of the answers that Job's so-called friends give him are technically true. But it is the "technical" part that ruins them. They are answers without personal relationship, intellect without intimacy. The answers are slapped onto Job's ravaged life like labels on a specimen bottle. Job rages against this secularized wisdom that has lost touch with the living realities of God.

Job defended himself:

> "I've had all I can take of your talk.
>   What a bunch of miserable comforters!
> Is there no end to your windbag speeches?
>   What's your problem that you go on and on like this?
> If you were in my shoes,
>   I could talk just like you.
> I could put together a terrific harangue
>   and really let you have it.
> But I'd never do that. I'd console and comfort,
>   make things better, not worse!" (Job 16:1-5)

In every generation there are men and women who pretend to be able to instruct us in a way of life that guarantees that we will be "healthy, wealthy, and wise." According to the propaganda of these people, anyone who lives intelligently and morally is exempt from suffering. From their point of view, it is lucky for us that they are now at hand to provide the intelligent and moral answers we need.

On behalf of all of us who have been misled by the platitudes of the nice people who show up to tell us everything is going to be just all right if we simply think such-and-such and do such-and-such, Job issues an anguished rejoinder. He rejects the kind of advice and teaching that has God all figured out, that provides glib explanations for every circumstance. Job's honest defiance continues to be the best defense against the clichés of positive thinkers and the prattle of religious small talk.

The honest, innocent Job is placed in a setting of immense suffering and then surrounded by the conventional religious wisdom of the day in the form of speeches by Eliphaz, Zophar, and Elihu. The contrast is unforgettable. The counselors methodically and pedantically recite their bookish precepts to Job. At first Job rages in pain and roars out his protests, but then he becomes silent in awestruck faith before God, who speaks from out of a storm—a "whirlwind" of Deity. Real faith cannot be reduced to spiritual bromides and merchandised in success stories. It is refined in the fires and the storms of pain.

The book of Job does not reject answers as such. There *is* content to biblical religion. It is the *secularization* of answers that is rejected —answers severed from their Source, the living God, the Word that both batters us and heals us. We cannot have truth *about* God divorced from the mind and heart *of* God.

In our compassion, we don't like to see people suffer. And so our instincts are aimed at preventing and alleviating suffering. No doubt that is a good impulse. But if we really want to reach out to others who are suffering, we should be careful not to be like Job's friends, not to do our "helping" with the presumption that we can fix things, get rid of them, or make them "better." We may look at our suffering friends and imagine how they could have better marriages, better-behaved children, better mental and emotional health. But when we rush in to fix suffering, we need to keep in mind several things.

First, no matter how insightful we may be, we don't *really* understand the full nature of our friends' problems. Second, our friends may not *want* our advice. Third, the ironic fact of the matter is that more often than not, people do not suffer *less* when they are committed to following God, but *more*. When these people go through suffering, their lives are often transformed, deepened, marked with beauty and holiness, in remarkable ways that could never have been anticipated before the suffering.

So, instead of continuing to focus on preventing suffering—which we simply won't be very successful at anyway—perhaps we should begin *entering* the suffering, participating insofar as we are able— entering the mystery and looking around for God. In other words, we need to quit feeling sorry for people who suffer and instead look up to them, learn from them, and — if they will let us — join them in protest and prayer. Pity can be nearsighted and condescending; shared suffering can be dignifying and life-changing. As we look at Job's suffering and praying and worshiping, we see that he has already blazed a trail of courage and integrity for us to follow.

But sometimes it's hard to know just how to follow Job's lead when we feel so alone in our suffering, unsure of what God wants us to do. What we must realize during those times of darkness is that the God who appeared to Job in the whirlwind is calling out to all of us. Although God may not appear to us in a vision, he makes himself known to us in all the many ways that he describes to Job — from the macro to the micro, from the wonders of the galaxies to the little things we take for granted. He is the Creator of the unfathomable universe all around us — and he is also the Creator of the universe inside of us.

GOD *answered Job. . . :*

"Where were you when I created the earth?
     Tell me since you know so much! . . .

"And have you ever ordered Morning, 'Get up!'
     told Dawn, 'Get to work!'
So you could seize Earth like a blanket
     and shake out the wicked like cockroaches? . . .

"Can you get the attention of the clouds,
     and commission a shower of rain?
Can you take charge of the lightning bolts
     and have them report to you for orders?" (Job 38:1, 4, 12-13, 34-35)

And so we gain hope — not from the darkness of our suffering, not from pat answers in books, but from the God who sees our suffering and shares our pain.

Reading Job prayerfully and meditatively leads us to face the questions that arise when our lives don't turn out the way we expect them to. First we hear all the stock answers. Then we ask the questions again, with variations — and hear the answers again, with variations. Over and over and over. Every time we let Job give voice to our own questions, our suffering gains in dignity and we are brought a step closer to the threshold of the voice and mystery of God. Every time we persist with Job in rejecting the quick-fix counsel of people who see us and hear us but do not understand us, we deepen our availability and openness to the revelation that comes only out of the tempest. The mystery of God eclipses the darkness and the struggle. We realize that suffering calls *our* lives into question, not God's. The tables are turned: God-Alive is present to us. God is speaking to us. And so Job's experience is confirmed and repeated once again in our suffering and our vulnerable humanity.

PSALMS

Conversation with a Holy God

Most Christians for most of the Christian centuries have learned to pray by praying the Psalms. The Hebrews, with several centuries of a head start on us in matters of prayer and worship, provided us with this prayer book that gives us a language adequate for responding to the God who speaks to us.

The stimulus to paraphrase the Psalms into a contemporary idiom comes from my lifetime of work as a pastor. As a pastor I was charged with, among other things, teaching people to pray, helping them to give voice to the entire experience of being human, and to do it both honestly and thoroughly. I found that it was not as easy as I expected. Getting started is easy enough. The impulse to pray is deep within us, at the very center of our created being, and so practically anything will do to get us started — "Help" and "Thanks!" are our basic prayers. But honesty and thoroughness don't come quite as spontaneously.

Faced with the prospect of conversation with a holy God who speaks worlds into being, it is not surprising that we have trouble. We feel awkward and out of place: "I'm not good enough for this. I'll wait until I clean up my act and prove that I am a decent person." Or we excuse ourselves on the grounds that our vocabulary is inadequate: "Give me a few months — or years! — to practice prayers that are polished enough for such a sacred meeting. Then I won't feel so stuttery and ill at ease."

My usual response when presented with these difficulties is to put the Psalms in a person's hand and say, "Go home and pray these. You've got wrong ideas about prayer; the praying you find in these Psalms will dispel the wrong ideas and introduce you to the real thing." A common response of those who do what I ask is surprise — they don't expect this kind of thing in the Bible. They're shocked to read Psalm 6:1-2: "Please, GOD, no more yelling, no more trips to the woodshed. Treat me nice for a change; I'm so starved for affection. Can't you see I'm black-and-blue, beat up badly in bones and soul? GOD, how long will it take for you to let up?" or Psalm 71:12-14: "God, don't just watch from the sidelines. Come on! Run to my side! My accusers — make them lose face. Those out to get me — make them look like idiots, while I stretch out, reaching for you, and daily add praise to praise." And then I express surprise at their surprise: "Did you think these would be the prayers of *nice* people? Did you think the psalmists' language would be polished and polite?"

Untutored, we tend to think that prayer is what good people do when they are doing their best. It is not. Inexperienced, we suppose that there must be an "insider" language that must be acquired before God takes us seriously in our prayer. There is not. Prayer is elemental, not advanced, language. It is the means by which our language becomes honest, true, and personal in response to God. It is the means by which we get everything in our lives out in the open before God. David wrote,

GOD, investigate my life;
　　get all the facts firsthand.
I'm an open book to you;
　　even from a distance, you know what I'm thinking. . . .

Investigate my life, O God,
　　find out everything about me;
Cross-examine and test me,
　　get a clear picture of what I'm about;
See for yourself whether I've done anything wrong —
　　then guide me on the road to eternal life. (Psalm 139:1,23-24)

But even with the Psalms in their hands and my pastoral encouragement, people often tell me that they still don't get it. In English translation, the Psalms often sound smooth and polished, sonorous with Elizabethan rhythms and diction. As literature, they are beyond compare. But as *prayer*, as the utterances of men and women passionate for God in moments of anger and praise and lament, these translations miss something. *Grammatically*, they are accurate. The scholarship undergirding the translations is superb and devout. But as *prayers* they are not quite right. The Psalms in Hebrew are earthy and rough. They are not genteel. They are not the prayers of nice people, couched in cultured language.

And so in my pastoral work of teaching people to pray, I started paraphrasing the Psalms into the rhythms and idiom of contemporary English. I wanted to provide men and women access to the immense range and the terrific energies of prayer in the kind of language that is most immediate to them, which also happens to be the language in which these psalm prayers were first expressed and written by David and his successors.

I continue to want to do that, convinced that only as we develop raw honesty and detailed thoroughness in our praying do we become whole, truly human in Jesus Christ, who also prayed the Psalms.

PROVERBS

The Art of Living Skillfully

Many people think that what's written in the Bible has mostly to do with getting people into heaven — getting right with God, saving their eternal souls. It does have to do with that, of course, but not mostly. It is equally concerned with living on this earth — living well, living in robust sanity. In our Scriptures, heaven is not the primary concern, to which earth is a tagalong afterthought. "On earth *as* it is in heaven" is Jesus' prayer.

"Wisdom" is the biblical term for this on-earth-as-it-is-in-heaven everyday living. Wisdom is the art of living skillfully in whatever actual conditions we find ourselves. It has virtually nothing to do with information as such, with knowledge as such. A college degree is no certification of wisdom — nor is it primarily concerned with keeping us out of moral mud puddles, although it does have a profound moral effect upon us. According to Proverbs 4:18-19, "The ways of right-living people glow with light; the longer they live, the brighter they shine. But the road of wrongdoing gets darker and darker — travelers can't see a thing; they fall flat on their faces."

Wisdom has to do with becoming skillful in honoring our parents and raising our children, handling our money and conducting our sexual lives, going to work and exercising leadership, using words well and treating friends kindly, eating and drinking healthily, cultivating emotions within ourselves and attitudes toward others that make for peace. Threaded through all these items is the insistence that the way we think of and respond to God is the most practical thing we do.

Trust GOD from the bottom of your heart;
*   don't try to figure out everything on your own.*
Listen for GOD's voice in everything you do, everywhere you go;
*   he's the one who will keep you on track.*
Don't assume that you know it all.
*   Run to GOD! Run from evil!*
Your body will glow with health,
*   your very bones will vibrate with life!*
Honor GOD with everything you own
*   give him the first and the best.*
Your barns will burst,
*   your wine vats will brim over.*
But don't, dear friend, resent GOD's discipline;
*   don't sulk under his loving correction.*
It's the child he loves that GOD corrects;
*   a father's delight is behind all this. (Proverbs 3:5-12)*

In matters of everyday practicality, nothing, absolutely nothing, takes precedence over God.

Proverbs concentrates on these concerns more than any other book in the Bible. Attention to the here and now is everywhere present in the stories and legislation, the prayers and the sermons, that are spread over the thousands of pages of the Bible. Proverbs distills it all into riveting images and aphorisms that keep us connected in holy obedience to the ordinary.

ECCLESIASTES

Experience of Futility

Unlike the animals, who seem quite content to simply be themselves, we humans are always looking for ways to be more than or other than what we find ourselves to be. We explore the countryside for excitement, search our souls for meaning, shop the world for pleasure. We try this. Then we try that. The usual fields of endeavor are money, sex, power, adventure, and knowledge.

Everything we try is so promising at first! But nothing ever seems to amount to very much. We intensify our efforts — but the harder we work at it, the less we get out of it. Some people give up early and settle for a humdrum life. Others never seem to learn, and so they flail away through a lifetime, becoming less and less human by the year, until by the time they die there is hardly enough humanity left to compose a corpse.

Ecclesiastes is a famous — maybe the world's most famous — witness to this experience of futility. The acerbic wit catches our attention. The stark honesty compels notice. And people do notice — oh, how they notice! Nonreligious and religious alike notice. Unbelievers and believers notice. More than a few of them are surprised to find this kind of thing in the Bible.

But it is most emphatically and necessarily in the Bible in order to call a halt to our various and futile attempts to make something of our lives, so that we can give our full attention to God — who God is and what he does to make something of us. Ecclesiastes actually doesn't say that much about God; the author leaves that to the other sixty-five books of the Bible. His task is to expose our total incapacity to find the meaning and completion of our lives on our own.

Smoke, nothing but smoke. [That's what the Quester says.]
  There's nothing to anything — it's all smoke.
What's there to show for a lifetime of work,
  a lifetime of working your fingers to the bone?
One generation goes its way, the next one arrives,
  but nothing changes — it's business as usual for old planet earth.
The sun comes up and the sun goes down,
  then does it again, and again — the same old round.
The wind blows south, the wind blows north.
  Around and around and around it blows,
  blowing this way, then that — the whirling, erratic wind.
All the rivers flow into the sea,
  but the sea never fills up.
The rivers keep flowing to the same old place,
  and then start all over and do it again.
Everything's boring, utterly boring —
  no one can find any meaning in it.
Boring to the eye,
  boring to the ear.
What was will be again,
  what happened will happen again.
There's nothing new on this earth.
  Year after year it's the same old thing.
Does someone call out, "Hey, this is *new"?*
  Don't get excited — it's the same old story.
Nobody remembers what happened yesterday.
  And the things that will happen tomorrow?
Nobody'll remember them either.
  Don't count on being remembered. (Ecclesiastes 1:2-11)

It is our propensity to go off on our own, trying to be human by our own devices and desires, that makes Ecclesiastes necessary reading. Ecclesiastes sweeps our souls clean of all "lifestyle" spiritu-alities so that we can be ready for God's visitation revealed in Jesus Christ. Ecclesiastes is a John-the-Baptist kind of book. It functions not as a meal but as a bath. It is not nourishment; it is cleansing. It is repentance. It is purging. We read Ecclesiastes to get scrubbed clean from illusion and sentiment, from ideas that are idolatrous and feel-ings that cloy. It is an exposé and rejection of every arrogant and igno-rant expectation that we can live our lives by ourselves on our own terms.

> *The words of the wise prod us to live well.*
> *They're like nails hammered home, holding life together.*
> *They are given by God, the one Shepherd.*
>
> *But regarding anything beyond this, dear friend, go easy.*
> *There's no end to the publishing of books, and constant study wears you*
> *out so you're no good for anything else. The last and final word is this:*
>   *Fear God.*
>   *Do what he tells you.*
>
> *And that's it. Eventually God will bring everything that*
> *we do out into the open and judge it according to its hidden intent,*
> *whether it's good or evil. (Ecclesiastes 12:11-14)*

Ecclesiastes challenges the naive optimism that sets a goal that appeals to us and then goes after it with gusto, expecting the result to be a good life. The author's cool skepticism, a refreshing negation to the lush and seductive suggestions swirling around us, promising everything but delivering nothing, clears the air. And once the air is cleared, we are ready for reality — for God.

["Ecclesiastes" is a Greek word that is usually translated "the Preacher" or "the Teacher." Because of the experiential stance of the writing in this book, giving voice to what is so basic among men and women throughout history, I have translated it "the Quester."]

SONG OF SONGS

An Integrated Wholeness

We don't read very far in the Song of Songs before we realize two things: one, it contains exquisite love lyrics, and two, it is very explicit sexually. The Song, in other words, makes a connection between conjugal love and sex — a very important and very biblical connection to make. There are some who would eliminate sex when they speak of love, supposing that they are making it more holy. Others, when they think of sex, never think of love. The Song proclaims an integrated wholeness that is at the center of Christian teaching on committed, wedded love for a world that seems to specialize in loveless sex.

The Song is a convincing witness that men and women were created physically, emotionally, and spiritually to live in love. At the outset of Scripture we read, "It is not good for man to live alone." The Song of Songs elaborates on the Genesis story by celebrating the union of two diverse personalities in love. Yet, even in their diversity, they agree:

[THE WOMAN:] *My dear lover glows with health —*
  red-blooded, radiant!
He's one in a million.
  There's no one quite like him! . . .
Everything about him delights me, thrills me through and through!
  (Song of Songs 5:10,16)
[THE MAN:] *There's no one like her on earth,*
  never has been, never will be.
She's a woman beyond compare.
  My dove is perfection. (Song of Songs 6:8-9)

We read Genesis and learn that this is the created pattern of joy and mutuality. We read the Song and see the goal and ideal toward which we all press for fulfillment. Despite our sordid failures in love, we see here what we are created for, what God intends for us in the ecstasy and fulfillment that is celebrated in the lyricism of the Song.

> *Love is invincible facing danger and death.*
>> *Passion laughs at the terrors of hell.*
> *The fire of love stops at nothing —*
>> *it sweeps everything before it.*
> *Flood waters can't drown love,*
>> *torrents of rain can't put it out.*
> *Love can't be bought, love can't be sold —*
>> *it's not to be found in the marketplace. (Song of Songs 8:6-7)*

Christians read the Song on many levels: as the intimacy of marital love between man and woman, God's deep love for his people, Christ's Bridegroom love for his church, the Christian's love for his or her Lord. It is a prism in which all the love of God in all the world, and all the responses of those who love and whom God loves, gathers and then separates into individual colors.

THE PROPHETS

EVERY NOOK AND CRANNY

O ver a period of several hundred years, the Hebrew people gave birth to an extraordinary number of prophets — men and women distinguished by the power and skill with which they presented the reality of God. They delivered God's commands and promises and living presence to communities and nations who had been living on god-fantasies and god-lies.

Everyone more or less believes in God. But most of us do our best to keep God on the margins of our lives or, failing that, refashion God to suit our convenience. Prophets insist that God is the sovereign center, not off in the wings awaiting our beck and call. Isaiah reminds us God is the "Amazing Counselor, Strong God, Eternal Father, Prince of Wholeness (Isaiah 9:6); Jeremiah says, "GOD is the real thing — the living God, the eternal King" (Jeremiah 10:10); Daniel calls him the "Revealer of Mysteries" (Daniel 2:29); Jonah notes that God is "sheer grace and mercy, not easily angered, rich in love, and ready at the drop of a hat to turn your plans of punishment into a program of forgiveness!" (Jonah 4:2); Nahum tells his readers, "GOD is serious business" (Nahum 1:2); and Habakkuk reminds us God is "from eternity," "Holy," and "Rock-Solid" (Habakkuk 1:12). And prophets insist that we deal with God as God reveals himself, not as we imagine him to be.

These men and women woke people up to the sovereign presence of God in their lives. They yelled, they wept, they rebuked, they soothed, they challenged, they comforted. They used words with power and imagination, whether blunt or subtle.

Sixteen of these prophets wrote what they spoke. We call them "the writing prophets." They comprise the section from Isaiah to Malachi in the Bible. These Hebrew prophets provide the help we so badly need if we are to stay alert and knowledgeable regarding the conditions in which we cultivate faithful and obedient lives before God. For the ways of the world — its assumptions, its values, its methods of going about its work — are never on the side of God. Never.

The prophets purge our imaginations of this world's assumptions on how life is lived and what counts in life. Micah wrote,

> *He's already made it plain how to live, what to do,*
> *what GOD is looking for in men and women.*
> *It's quite simple: Do what is fair and just to your neighbor,*
> *be compassionate and loyal in your love,*
> *And don't take yourself too seriously —*
> *take God seriously. (Micah 6:8)*

Over and over again, God the Holy Spirit uses these prophets to separate his people from the cultures in which they live, putting them back on the path of simple faith and obedience and worship in defiance of all that the world admires and rewards. Prophets train us in discerning the difference between the ways of the world and the ways of the gospel, keeping us present to the Presence of God.

We don't read very many pages into the Prophets before realizing that there was nothing easygoing about them. Prophets were not popular figures. They never achieved celebrity status. They were decidedly uncongenial to the temperaments and dispositions of the people with whom they lived. And the centuries have not mellowed them. It's understandable that we should have a difficult time coming to terms with them. They aren't particularly sensitive to our feelings. They have very modest, as we would say, "relationship skills." We like leaders, especially religious leaders, who understand our problems ("come alongside us" is our idiom for it), leaders with a touch of glamour, leaders who look good on posters and on television.

The hard-rock reality is that prophets don't fit into our way of life.

For a people who are accustomed to "fitting God" into their lives, or, as we like to say, "making room for God," the prophets are hard to take and easy to dismiss. The God of whom the prophets speak is far too large to fit into our lives. If we want anything to do with God, we have to fit into him. Isaiah reminds us,

"I don't think the way you think.
  The way you work isn't the way I work."
    GOD's *Decree.*
"For as the sky soars high above earth,
  so the way I work surpasses the way you work,
  and the way I think is beyond the way you think." (Isaiah 55:8-9)

The prophets are not "reasonable," accommodating themselves to what makes sense to us. They are not diplomatic, tactfully negotiating an agreement that allows us a "say" in the outcome. What they do is haul us unceremoniously into a reality far too large to be accounted for by our explanations and expectations. They plunge us into mystery, immense and staggering.

Their words and visions penetrate the illusions with which we cocoon ourselves from reality. We humans have an enormous capacity for denial and self-deceit. We incapacitate ourselves from dealing with the consequences of sin, for facing judgment, for embracing truth. Then the prophets step in and help us to first recognize and then enter the new life God has for us, the life that hope in God opens up. Jeremiah spoke "God's Word on the subject: . . . 'I know what I'm doing. I have it all planned out — plans to take care of you, not abandon you, plans to give you the future you hope for'" (Jeremiah 29:11). And Micah led by example: "But me, I'm not giving up. I'm sticking around to see what God will do. I'm waiting for God to make things right. I'm counting on God to listen to me" (Micah 7:7).

They don't explain God. They shake us out of the old conventional habits of small-mindedness, of trivializing god-gossip, and set us on our feet in wonder and obedience and worship. If we insist on understanding them before we live into them, we will never get it.

Basically, the prophets did two things: They worked to get people to accept the worst as *God's* judgment — not a religious catastrophe or a political disaster, but *judgment*. If what seems like the worst turns out to be *God's* judgment, it can be embraced, not denied or avoided, for God is good and intends our salvation. So judgment, while certainly not what we human beings anticipate in our planned future, can never be the worst that can happen. It is the best, for it is the work of God to set the world, and us, right.

And the prophets worked to get people who were beaten down to open themselves up to hope in God's future. In the wreckage of exile and death and humiliation and sin, the prophets ignited hope, opening lives to the new work of salvation that God is about at all times and everywhere. Through Isaiah, God said,

"Pay attention, my people.
Listen to me, nations.
Revelation flows from me.
My decisions light up the world.
My deliverance arrives on the run,
my salvation right on time.
I'll bring justice to the peoples.
Even faraway islands will look to me
and take hope in my saving power.
Look up at the skies,
ponder the earth under your feet.
The skies will fade out like smoke,
the earth will wear out like work pants,
and the people will die off like flies.
But my salvation will last forever,
my setting-things-right will never be obsolete." (Isaiah 51:4-6)

One of the bad habits that we pick up early in our lives is separating things and people into secular and sacred. We assume that the secular is what we are more or less in charge of: our jobs, our time, our entertainment, our government, our social relations. The sacred is what God has charge of: worship and the Bible, heaven and hell, church and prayers. We then contrive to set aside a sacred place for God, designed, we say, to honor God but really intended to keep God in his place, leaving us free to have the final say about everything else that goes on.

Prophets will have none of this. They contend that everything, absolutely everything, takes place on sacred ground. God has something to say about every aspect of our lives: The way we feel and act in the so-called privacy of our hearts and homes, the way we make our money and the way we spend it, the politics we embrace, the wars we fight, the catastrophes we endure, the people we hurt and the people we help. Nothing is hidden from the scrutiny of God, nothing is exempt from the rule of God, nothing escapes the purposes of God. Holy, holy, holy.

Prophets make it impossible to evade God or make detours around God. Prophets insist on receiving God in every nook and cranny of life. For a prophet, God is more real than the next-door neighbor.

ISAIAH

The Salvation Symphony

For Isaiah, words are watercolors and melodies and chisels to make truth and beauty and goodness. Or, as the case may be, hammers and swords and scalpels to *unmake* sin and guilt and rebellion. Isaiah does not merely convey information. He creates visions, delivers revelation, arouses belief. He is a poet in the most fundamental sense — a *maker*, making God present and that presence urgent. Isaiah is the supreme poet-prophet to come out of the Hebrew people.

Isaiah is a large presence in the lives of people who live by faith in God, who submit themselves to being shaped by the Word of God and are on the lookout for the holy. *The Holy.* The characteristic name for God in Isaiah is "The Holy." As we read this large and comprehensive gathering of messages that were preached to the ancient people of Israel, we find ourselves immersed in both the presence and the action of The Holy: "By working justice, God-of-the-Angel-Armies will be a mountain. By working righteousness, Holy God will show what 'holy' is" (Isaiah 5:16).

The more hours we spend pondering the words of Isaiah, the more the word "holy" changes in our understanding. If "holy" was ever a pious, pastel-tinted word in our vocabularies, the Isaiah-preaching quickly turns it into something blazing. Holiness is the most attractive quality, the most intense experience we ever get of sheer *life* — authentic, firsthand living, not life looked at and enjoyed from a distance. We find ourselves in on the operations of God himself, not talking about them or reading about them. Holiness is a furnace that transforms the men and women who enter it. So,

"Who among us can survive this firestorm?
Who of us can get out of this purge with our lives?"

The answer's simple:
Live right,
speak the truth,
despise exploitation,
refuse bribes,
reject violence,
avoid evil amusements.
This is how you raise your standard of living!
A safe and stable way to live.
A nourishing, satisfying way to live. (Isaiah 33:14-16)

"Holy, Holy, Holy" is not needlepoint. It is the banner of a revolution, *the* revolution.

The book of Isaiah is expansive, dealing with virtually everything that is involved in being a people of God on this planet Earth. The impressive art of Isaiah involves taking the stuff of our ordinary and often disappointing human experience and showing us how it is the very stuff that God uses to create and save and give hope. As this vast panorama opens up before us, it turns out that nothing is unusable by God. He uses everything and everybody as material for his work, which is the remaking of the mess we have made of our lives.

"Count on it: Everyone who had it in for you
will end up out in the cold —
real losers.
Those who worked against you
will end up empty-handed —

nothing to show for their lives.
When you go out looking for your old adversaries
    you won't find them —
Not a trace of your old enemies,
    not even a memory.
That's right. Because I, your GOD,
    have a firm grip on you and I'm not letting go.
I'm telling you, 'Don't panic.
    I'm right here to help you.'"(Isaiah 41:11-13)

"Symphony" is the term many find useful to capture the fusion of simplicity and complexity presented in the book of Isaiah. The major thrust is clearly God's work of salvation: "The Salvation Symphony" (the name Isaiah means "God Saves"). The prominent themes repeated and developed throughout this vast symphonic work are judgment, comfort, and hope. All three elements are present on nearly every page, but each also gives distinction to the three "movements" of the book that so powerfully enact salvation: Messages of Judgment (chapters 1–39), Messages of Comfort (chapters 40–55), and Messages of Hope (chapters 56–66).

JEREMIAH

God-Revealing Companion

Jeremiah's life and Jeremiah's book are a single piece. He wrote what he lived, he lived what he wrote. There is no dissonance between his life and his book. Some people write better than they live; others live better than they write. Jeremiah, writing or living, was the same Jeremiah.

This is important to know because Jeremiah is the prophet of choice for many when we find ourselves having to live through difficult times and want some trustworthy help in knowing what to think, how to pray, how to carry on. We'd like some verification of credentials. This book provides the verification.

We live in disruptive times. The decades preceding and following the pivotal third millennium are not exactly unprecedented. There have certainly been comparable times of disruption in the past that left everyone reeling, wondering what on earth and in heaven was going on. But whatever their occasion or size, troubles require attention.

Jeremiah's troubled life spanned one of the most troublesome periods in Hebrew history, the decades leading up to the fall of Jerusalem in 587 B.C., followed by the Babylonian exile. Everything that could go wrong *did* go wrong. And Jeremiah was in the middle of all of it, sticking it out, praying and preaching, suffering and striving, writing and believing. He lived through crushing storms of hostility and furies of bitter doubt. Every muscle in his body was stretched to the limit by fatigue; every thought in his mind was subjected to questioning; every feeling in his heart was put through fires of ridicule. He experienced it all agonizingly and wrote it all magnificently.

You pushed me into this, GOD, and I let you do it.
>   You were too much for me.
And now I'm a public joke.
>   They all poke fun at me.
Every time I open my mouth
>   I'm shouting, "Murder!" or "Rape!"
And all I get for my God-warnings
>   are insults and contempt.
But if I say, "Forget it!
>   No more GOD-Messages from me!"
The words are fire in my belly
>   a burning in my bones.
I'm worn out trying to hold it in.
>   I can't do it any longer!
Then I hear whispering behind my back:
>   "There goes old 'Danger-Everywhere.' Shut him up! Report him!"
Old friends watch, hoping I'll fall flat on my face:
>   "One misstep and we'll have him. We'll get rid of him for good!"

But GOD, a most fierce warrior, is at my side.
>   Those who are after me will be sent sprawling —
Slapstick buffoons falling all over themselves,
>   a spectacle of humiliation no one will ever forget.

Oh, GOD-of-the-Angel-Armies, no one fools you.
>   You see through everyone, everything.
I want to see you pay them back for what they've done.
>   I rest my case with you.

Sing to GOD! All praise to GOD!
>   He saves the weak from the grip of the wicked. (Jeremiah 20:7-13)

What happens when everything you believe in and live by is smashed to bits by circumstances? Sometimes the reversals of what we expect from God come to us as individuals, other times as entire communities. When it happens, does catastrophe work to re-form our lives to conform to who God actually is and not the way we imagined or wished him to be? Does it lead to an abandonment of God? Or, worse, does it trigger a stubborn grasping to the old collapsed system of belief, holding on for dear life to an illusion?

Anyone who lives in disruptive times looks for companions who have been through them earlier, wanting to know how they went through it, how they made it, what it was like. In looking for a companion who has lived through catastrophic disruption and survived with grace, biblical people more often than not come upon Jeremiah and receive him as a true, honest, and God-revealing companion for the worst of times, who reassures us that, no matter what, God has "never quit loving you and never will" (Jeremiah 31:3).

LAMENTATIONS

Witness to Suffering

Lamentations is a concentrated and intense biblical witness to suffering. Suffering is a huge, unavoidable element in the human condition. To be human is to suffer. No one gets an exemption. It comes as no surprise then to find that our Holy Scriptures, immersed as they are in the human condition, provide extensive witness to suffering.

There are two polar events in the history of the Hebrew people: the Exodus from Egypt and the Exile into Babylon. Exodus is the definitive story of salvation into a free life. God delivered his people from Egyptian slavery (in about 1200 B.C.). It is a story of freedom. It's accompanied by singing and dancing — an exuberant experience. Exile is the definitive story of judgment accompanied by immense suffering. God's people are taken into Babylonian slavery (the fall of Jerusalem in 587 B.C. marks the event). It is a time of devastation and lament. It is a terrible experience. The two events, Exodus and Exile, are bookends holding together the wide-ranging experiences of God's people that fall between the exuberance that accompanies salvation and the suffering associated with judgment.

Lamentations, written out of the Exile experience, provides the community of faith with a form and vocabulary for dealing with loss and pain. The precipitating event, the fall of Jerusalem, is told in 2 Kings 25 and Jeremiah 52. It is impossible to overstate either the intensity or the complexity of the suffering that came to a head in the devastation of Jerusalem and then continued on into the seventy years of exile in Babylon. Lamentations 1:7 says, "Jerusalem remembers the day she lost everything, when her people fell into enemy hands, and not a soul there to help. Enemies looked on and laughed, laughed at her helpless silence." Loss was total. Carnage was rampant. Cannibalism and sacrilege were twin horrors stalking the streets of destroyed Jerusalem. The desperate slaying of innocent children showed complete loss of respect for human worth, and the angry murder of priests showed absolute loss of respect for divine will. The worst that can happen to body and spirit, to person and nation, happened here—a nadir of suffering. And throughout the world the suffering continues, both in large-scale horrors and in personal agonies.

Neither explaining suffering nor offering a program for the elimination of suffering, Lamentations keeps company with the extensive biblical witness that gives dignity to suffering by insisting that God enters our suffering and is companion to our suffering.

> GOD's loyal love couldn't have run out,
>   his merciful love couldn't have dried up.
> They're created new every morning.
>   How great your faithfulness!
> I'm sticking with GOD (I say it over and over).
>   He's all I've got left.
>
> God proves to be good to the man who passionately waits,
>   to the woman who diligently seeks.
> It's a good thing to quietly hope,
>   quietly hope for help from GOD. . . .
>
> When life is heavy and hard to take,
>   go off by yourself. Enter the silence.
> Bow in prayer. Don't ask questions:
>   Wait for hope to appear.
> Don't run from trouble. Take it full-face.
>   The "worst" is never the worst.

Why? Because the Master won't ever
    walk out and fail to return.
If he works severely, he also works tenderly.
    His stockpiles of loyal love are immense.
He takes no pleasure in making life hard,
    in throwing roadblocks in the way. (Lamentations 3:22-33)

EZEKIEL

Master at Dealing with Catastrophe

Catastrophe strikes and a person's world falls apart. People respond variously, but two of the more common responses are denial and despair. Denial refuses to acknowledge the catastrophe. It shuts its eyes tight or looks the other way; it manages to act as if everything is going to be just fine; it takes refuge in distractions and lies and fantasies. Despair is paralyzed by the catastrophe and accepts it as the end of the world. It is unwilling to do anything, concluding that life for all intents and purposes is over. Despair listlessly closes its eyes to a world in which all the color has drained out, a world gone dead.

Among biblical writers, Ezekiel is our master at dealing with catastrophe. When catastrophe struck — it was the sixth-century B.C. invasion of Israel by Babylon — denial was the primary response. Ezekiel found himself living among a people of God who (astonishingly similar to us!) stubbornly refused to see what was right before their eyes (the denial crowd). There were also some who were unwilling to see anything other than what was right before their eyes (the despair crowd).

But Ezekiel saw. He saw what the people with whom he lived either couldn't or wouldn't see. He saw in wild and unforgettable images, elaborated in exuberant detail — God at work in a catastrophic era: fearsome creatures (Ezekiel 1), an edible book (Ezekiel 2), bones coming to life (Ezekiel 37:1-14). The denial people refused to see that the catastrophe was in fact catastrophic. How could it be? God wouldn't let anything that bad happen to them. Ezekiel showed them. He showed them that, yes, there *was* catastrophe, but God was at work in the catastrophe, sovereignly *using* the catastrophe. He showed them so that they would be able to embrace God in the worst of times.

The despair people, overwhelmed by the devastation, refused to see that life was worth living. How could it be? They had lost everything, or would soon — country, Temple, freedom, and many, many lives. Ezekiel showed them. He showed them that God was and would be at work in the wreckage and rubble, sovereignly *using* the disaster to create a new people of God.

"This is your Message from GOD, the Master. True, I sent you to the far country and scattered you through other lands. All the same, I've provided you a temporary sanctuary in the countries where you've gone. I will gather you back from those countries and lands where you've been scattered and give you back the land of Israel. You'll come back and clean house, throw out all the rotten images and obscene idols. I'll give you a new heart. I'll put a new spirit in you. I'll cut out your stone heart and replace it with a red-blooded, firm-muscled heart. Then you'll obey my statutes and be careful to obey my commands. You'll be my people! I'll be your God!" (Ezekiel 11:16-20)

Whether through denial or despair, the people of God nearly lost their identity as a people of God. But they didn't. God's people emerged from that catastrophic century robust and whole. And the reason, in large part, was Ezekiel.

DANIEL

Wide Screen Rendition of God's Sovereignty

Images generated by the book of Daniel have been percolating through the daily experiences of the people of God for well over two thousand years now, producing a richly aromatic brew stimulating God's people to obey and trust their sovereign God.

Obedience to God in the pressures and stresses of day-by-day living and trust in God's ways in the large sweep of history are always at risk, but especially in times of suffering and persecution. Obedience to God is difficult when we are bullied into compliance to the God-ignoring culture out of sheer survival. Trust in God is likewise at risk of being abandoned in favor of the glamorous seductions of might and size.

Daniel was written out of just such times. There was little or no observable evidence in the circumstances to commend against-the-stream obedience or overarching trust. But Daniel's stories and visions have supplied what that society did not — could not — give. Century after century, Daniel has shot adrenaline into the veins of God-obedience and put backbone into God-trust, saying,

> "Blessed be the name of God,
>   forever and ever.
> He knows all, does all:
>   He changes the seasons and guides history,
> He raises up kings and also brings them down,
>   he provides both intelligence and discernment,
> He opens up the depths, tells the secrets,
>   sees in the dark — light spills out of him!" (Daniel 2:20-22)

Daniel is composed, in approximately equal parts, of stories and visions — six stories (chapters 1–6) and four visions (chapters 7–12). The stories tell of souls living faithfully in obedience to God in a time of adversity. The visions are wide-screen renditions of God's sovereignty worked out among nations who couldn't care less about him. Six soul stories; four sovereignty visions.

The six soul-survival stories nourish a commitment to integrity and perseverance right now. Very few of us live in settings congenial to God-loyalty and among people who affirm a costly discipleship. Hardly a day goes by that we do not have to choose between compliance to what is expedient and loyalty to our Lord. The stories keep us alert to what is at stake day by day, hour by hour.

The four visions of God's history-saving ways nourish hope in God during times when world events seem to put God in eclipse. The visions are difficult to understand, written as they are in a deliberately cryptic style (apocalyptic). From time to time they have been subjected to intense study and explanation. But for a first reading, perhaps it is better simply to let the strange symbolic figures give witness to the large historical truth that eclipses the daily accumulation of historical facts reported by our news media, namely, that God is sovereign. In the course of all the noise and shuffling, strutting and posing, of arrogant rulers and nations that we call history, with the consequent troubles to us all, God is serenely sovereign; we can trust him to bring all things and people under his rule. In Daniel, even the mighty king Nebuchadnezzar came to admit there was a power greater than his. He said of God,

"His sovereign rule lasts and lasts,
    his kingdom never declines and falls.
Life on this earth doesn't add up to much,
    but God's heavenly army keeps everything going.

No one can interrupt his work,
  no one can call his rule into question. . . .

Everything he does is right,
  and he does it the right way.
He knows how to turn a proud person
  into a humble man or woman." (Daniel 4:34-35,37)

There are always some of us who want to concentrate on the soul, and others of us who want to deal with the big issues of history. Daniel is one of our primary documents for keeping it all together — the personal and the political, the present and the future, the soul and society.

HOSEA

A Lived Parable

We live in a world awash in love stories. Most of them are lies. They are not love stories at all — they are lust stories, sex-fantasy stories, domination stories. From the cradle we are fed on lies about love.

This would be bad enough if it only messed up human relationships — man and woman, parent and child, friend and friend — but it also messes up God-relationships. The huge, mountainous reality of all existence is that God is love, that God loves the world. Each single detail of the real world that we face and deal with day after day is permeated by this love.

But when our minds and imaginations are crippled with lies about love, we have a hard time understanding this fundamental ingredient of daily living, "love," either as a noun or as a verb. And if the basic orienting phrase "God is love" is plastered over with cultural graffiti that obscure and deface the truth of the way the world is, we are not going to get very far in living well. We require true stories of love if we are to live truly.

Hosea is the prophet of love, but not love as we imagine or fantasize it. He was a parable of God's love for his people lived out as God revealed and enacted it — a lived parable. It is an astonishing story: a prophet commanded to marry a common whore and have children with her. It is an even more astonishing message: God loves us in just this way — goes after us at our worst, keeps after us until he gets us, and makes lovers of men and women who know nothing of real love. He says,

"*I will heal their waywardness.*
   I will love them lavishly. My anger is played out.

I will make a fresh start with Israel.
 He'll burst into bloom like a crocus in the spring.
He'll put down deep oak tree roots,
 he'll become a forest of oaks!
He'll become splendid — like a giant sequoia,
 his fragrance like a grove of cedars!
Those who live near him will be blessed by him,
 be blessed and prosper like golden grain.
Everyone will be talking about them,
 spreading their fame as the vintage children of God.
Ephraim is finished with gods that are no-gods.
 From now on I'm the one who answers and satisfies him.
I am like a luxuriant fruit tree.
 Everything you need is to be found in me." (Hosea 14:4-8)

Once we absorb this story and the words that flow from it, we will know God far more accurately. And we will be well on our way to being cured of all the sentimentalized and neurotic distortions of love that incapacitate us from dealing with the God who loves us and loving the neighbors who don't love us.

JOEL

Decision Valley

When disaster strikes, understanding of God is at risk. Unexpected illness or death, national catastrophe, social disruption, personal loss, plague or epidemic, devastation by flood or drought, turn men and women who haven't given God a thought in years into instant theologians. Rumors fly: "God is absent" . . . "God is angry" . . . "God is playing favorites, and I'm not the favorite" . . . "God is ineffectual" . . . "God is holding a grudge from a long time ago, and now we're paying for it" . . .

It is the task of the prophet to stand up at such moments of catastrophe and clarify who God is and how he acts. If the prophet is good—that is, accurate and true—the disaster becomes a lever for prying people's lives loose from their sins and setting them free for God. Joel is one of the good ones: He used a current event in Israel as a text to call his people to an immediate awareness that there wasn't a day that went by that they weren't dealing with God. We are always dealing with God.

The event that Joel used as his text was a terrible locust plague that was devastating the crops of Israel, creating an agricultural disaster of major proportions. He compared it to a massive military invasion.

The locust army seems all horses —
galloping horses, an army of horses.
It sounds like thunder
leaping on mountain ridges,
Or like the roar of wildfire
through grass and brush,

Or like an invincible army shouting for blood,
    ready to fight, straining at the bit.
At the sight of this army,
    the people panic, faces white with terror. (Joel 2:4-6)

But any catastrophe would have served him as well. He projected it onto a big screen and used it to focus the reality of God in the lives of his people. Then he expanded the focus to include everything and everyone *everywhere* — the whole world crowded into Decision Valley for God's verdict. This powerful picture has kept God's people alert to the eternal consequences of their decisions for many centuries.

There is a sense in which catastrophe doesn't introduce anything new into our lives. It simply exposes the moral or spiritual reality that already exists but was hidden beneath an overlay of routine, self-preoccupation, and business as usual. Then suddenly, there it is before us: a moral universe in which our accumulated decisions — on what we say and do, on how we treat others, on whether or not we will obey God's commands — are set in the stark light of God's judgment.

In our everyday experience, right and wrong and the decisions we make about them seldom come to us neatly packaged and precisely defined. Joel's prophetic words continue to reverberate down through the generations, making the ultimate connection between anything, small or large, that disrupts our daily routine, and God, giving us fresh opportunity to reorient our lives in faithful obedience.

It's not too late —
    GOD's personal Message —
"Come back to me and really mean it!
    Come fasting and weeping, sorry for your sins!"
Change your life, not just your clothes.

Come back to GOD, *your God.*
And here's why: God is kind and merciful.
He takes a deep breath, puts up with a lot,
This most patient God, extravagant in love,
always ready to cancel catastrophe.
Who knows? Maybe he'll do it now,
maybe he'll turn around and show pity.
Maybe, when all's said and done,
there'll be blessings full and robust for your GOD! *(Joel 2:12-14)*

Joel gives us opportunity for "deathbed repentance" before we die, while there is still time and space for a lot of good living to the glory of God.

AMOS

Defender of the Downtrodden

More people are exploited and abused in the cause of religion than in any other way. Sex, money, and power all take a backseat to religion as a source of evil. Religion is the most dangerous energy source known to humankind. The moment a person (or government or religion or organization) is convinced that God is either ordering or sanctioning a cause or project, anything goes. The history, worldwide, of religion-fueled hate, killing, and oppression is staggering. The biblical prophets are in the front line of those doing something about it.

The biblical prophets continue to be the most powerful and effective voices ever heard on this earth for keeping religion honest, humble, and compassionate. Prophets sniff out injustice, especially injustice that is dressed up in religious garb. They sniff it out a mile away. Prophets see through hypocrisy, especially hypocrisy that assumes a religious pose. Prophets are not impressed by position or power or authority. They aren't taken in by numbers, size, or appearances of success.

They pay little attention to what men and women say about God or do for God. They listen to God and rigorously test all human language and action against what they hear. Among these prophets, Amos towers as defender of the downtrodden poor and accuser of the powerful rich who use God's name to legitimize their sin.

People hate this kind of talk.
  Raw truth is never popular.
But here it is, bluntly spoken:
  Because you run roughshod over the poor

and take the bread right out of their mouths,
    You're never going to move into
        the luxury homes you have built.
You're never going to drink wine
        from the expensive vineyards you've planted.
I know precisely the extent of your violations,
        the enormity of your sins. Appalling!
You bully right-living people,
        taking bribes right and left and kicking the poor when they're down.

Justice is a lost cause. Evil is epidemic.
        Decent people throw up their hands.
Protest and rebuke are useless,
        a waste of breath.

Seek good and not evil —
        and live!
You talk about GOD, *the God-of-the-Angel-Armies,*
        being your best friend.
Well, live *like it,*
        and maybe it will happen.

Hate evil and love good,
        then work it out in the public square.
Maybe GOD, *the God-of-the-Angel-Armies,*
        will notice your remnant and be gracious. (Amos 5:10-15)

None of us can be trusted in this business. If we pray and worship God and associate with others who likewise pray and worship God, we absolutely must keep company with these biblical prophets. We are required to submit all our words and acts to their passionate scrutiny to prevent the perversion of our religion into something self-serving.

A spiritual life that doesn't give a large place to the prophet-articulated justice will end up making us worse instead of better, separating us from God's ways instead of drawing us into them.

OBADIAH

A New Vocation

It takes the entire Bible to read any part of the Bible. Even the brief walk-on appearance of Obadiah has its place. No one, whether in or out of the Bible, is without significance. It was Obadiah's assignment to give voice to God's word of judgment against Edom.

Back in the early stages of the biblical narrative, we are told the story of the twins Jacob and Esau (Genesis 25–36). They came out of the womb fighting. Jacob was ancestor to the people of Israel, Esau ancestor to the people of Edom. The two neighboring peoples, Israel mostly to the west of the Jordan River and Dead Sea and Edom to the southeast, never did get along. They had a long history of war and rivalry. When Israel was taken into exile — first the northern king-dom by the Assyrians in 721 B.C. and later the southern kingdom by the Babylonians in 586 B.C. — Edom stood across the fence and watched, glad to see her old relative get beat up. God, however, was not pleased.

> Godless foreigners invaded and pillaged Jerusalem.
>   You stood there and watched.
>   You were as bad as they were.
> You shouldn't have gloated over your brother
>   when he was down-and-out.
> You shouldn't have laughed and joked at Judah's sons
>   when they were facedown in the mud.
> You shouldn't have talked so big
>   when everything was so bad.

You shouldn't have taken advantage of my people
    when their lives had fallen apart. . . .

"GOD's Judgment Day is near
    for all the godless nations.
As you have done, it will be done to you.
    What you did will boomerang back
    and hit your own head." (Obadiah 11-12,15)

At first reading, this brief but intense prophecy of Obadiah, targeted at Edom, is a broadside indictment of Edom's cruel injustice to God's chosen people. Edom is the villain and God's covenant people the victim.

But the last line of the prophecy takes a giant step out of the centuries of hate and rivalry and invective. Israel, so often a victim of Edomite aggression through the centuries, is suddenly revealed to be saved from the injustices of the past and taking up a position of rule over their ancient enemies the Edomites. But instead of doing to others what had been done to them and continuing the cycle of violence that they had been caught in, they are presented as taking over the reins of government and administering God's justice justly. They find themselves in a new context — God's kingdom — and realize that they have a new vocation — to represent God's rule. It is not much (one verse out of twenty-one!), but it is a glimmer (it *is* the final verse!).

The remnant of the saved in Mount Zion
    will go into the mountains of Esau
And rule justly and fairly,
    a rule that honors GOD's kingdom. (Obadiah 21)

On the Day of Judgment, dark retaliation and invective do not get the last word. Only the first rays of the light of justice appear here. But these rays will eventually add up to a kingdom of light, in which all nations will be judged justly from the eternal throne in heaven.

JONAH

A Companion in Our Ineptness

Everybody knows about Jonah. People who have never read the Bible know enough about Jonah to laugh at a joke about him and the "whale." Jonah has entered our folklore. There is a playful aspect to his story, a kind of slapstick clumsiness about Jonah as he bumbles his way along, trying, but always unsuccessfully, to avoid God. Jonah 1:3 says, "Jonah got up and went the other direction to Tarshish, running away from GOD. . . . as far away from GOD as he could get."

But the playfulness is not frivolous. This is deadly serious. While we are smiling or laughing at Jonah, we drop the guard with which we are trying to keep God at a comfortable distance, and suddenly we find ourselves caught in the purposes and commands of God. All of us. No exceptions.

Stories are the most prominent biblical way of helping us see ourselves in "the God story," which always gets around to the story of God making and saving us. Stories, in contrast to abstract statements of truth, tease us into becoming participants in what is being said. We find ourselves involved in the action. We may start out as spectators or critics, but if the story is good (and the biblical stories are very good!), we find ourselves no longer just listening to but inhabiting the story.

One reason that the Jonah story is so enduringly important for nurturing the life of faith in us is that Jonah is not a hero too high and mighty for us to identify with — he doesn't do anything great. Instead of being held up as an ideal to admire, we find Jonah as a companion in our ineptness. Here is someone on our level. Even when Jonah does it right (like preaching, finally, in Nineveh) he does it wrong (by getting angry at God). But the whole time, God is working within and around Jonah's very ineptness and accomplishing his purposes in him. Most of us need a biblical friend or two like Jonah.

MICAH

A Master of Metaphor

Prophets use words to remake the world. The world — heaven and earth, men and women, animals and birds — was made in the first place by God's Word. Prophets, arriving on the scene and finding that world in ruins, finding a world of moral rubble and spiritual disorder, take up the work of words again to rebuild what human disobedience and mistrust demolished. These prophets learn their speech from God. Their words are God-grounded, God-energized, God-passionate. As their words enter the language of our communities, men and women find themselves in the presence of God, who enters the mess of human sin to rebuke and renew.

> "On that great day," God says,
> "I will round up all the hurt and homeless,
> everyone I have bruised or banished.
> I will transform the battered into a company of the elite.
> I will make a strong nation out of the long lost,
> A showcase exhibit of God's rule in action,
> as I rule from Mount Zion, from here to eternity." (Micah 4:6-7)

Left to ourselves we turn God into an object, something we can deal with, some *thing* we can use to our benefit, whether that thing is a feeling or an idea or an image. Prophets scorn all such stuff. They train us to respond to God's presence and voice.

Micah, the final member of that powerful quartet of writing prophets who burst on the world scene in the eighth century B.C.

(Isaiah, Hosea, and Amos were the others), like virtually all his fellow prophets — those charged with keeping people alive to God and alert to listening to the voice of God — was a master of metaphor. This means that he used words not simply to define or identify what can be seen, touched, smelled, heard, or tasted, but to plunge us into a world of *presence*. To experience presence is to enter that far larger world of reality that our sensory experiences point to but cannot describe — the realities of love and compassion, justice and faithfulness, sin and evil . . . and God. Mostly God.

> *Where is the god who can compare with you —*
> > *wiping the slate clean of guilt,*
> *Turning a blind eye, a deaf ear,*
> > *to the past sins of your purged and precious people?*
> *You don't nurse your anger and don't stay angry long,*
> > *for mercy is your specialty. That's what you love most.*
> *And compassion is on its way to us.*
> > *You'll stamp out our wrongdoing.*
> *You'll sink our sins*
> > *to the bottom of the ocean.*
> *You'll stay true to your word to Father Jacob*
> > *and continue the compassion you showed Grandfather Abraham —*
> *Everything you promised our ancestors*
> > *from a long time ago. (Micah 7:18-20)*

The realities that are Word-evoked are where most of the world's action takes place. There are no "mere words."

Nahum

The Main Action: God!

The stage of history is large. Larger-than-life figures appear on this stage from time to time, swaggering about, brandishing weapons and money, terrorizing and bullying. These figures are not, as they suppose themselves to be, at the center of the stage — not, in fact, anywhere near the center. But they make a lot of noise and are able to call attention to themselves. They often manage to get a significant number of people watching and even admiring: big nations, huge armies, important people. At any given moment a few superpower nations and their rulers dominate the daily news. Every century a few of these names are left carved on its park benches, marking rather futile, and in retrospect pitiable, attempts at immortality.

The danger is that the noise of these pretenders to power will distract us from what is going on quietly at the center of the stage in the person and action of God. God's characteristic way of working is in quietness and through prayer. "I speak," says poet George Meredith, "of the unremarked forces that split the heart and make the pavement toss — forces concealed in quiet people and plants." If we are conditioned to respond to noise and size, we will miss God's word and action. However,

> God *is serious business.*
> > *He won't be trifled with.*
> *He avenges his foes.*
> > *He stands up against his enemies, fierce and raging.*
> *But* God *doesn't lose his temper.*
> > *He's powerful, but it's a patient power.*

Still, no one gets by with anything.
  Sooner or later, everyone pays. (Nahum 1:2-3)

From time to time, God assigns someone to pay attention to one
or another of these persons or nations or movements just long enough
to get the rest of us to *quit* paying so much attention to them and
get back to the main action: *God*! Nahum drew that assignment in
the seventh century B.C. Assyria had the whole world terrorized. At
the time that Nahum delivered his prophecy, Assyria (and its capital,
Nineveh) appeared invincible. A world free of Assyrian domination
was unimaginable. Nahum's task was to make it imaginable — to free
God's people from Assyrian paralysis, free them to believe in and pray
to a sovereign God. Nahum's preaching, his Spirit-born metaphors, his
God-shaped syntax, knocked Assyria off her high horse and cleared
the field of Nineveh-distraction so that Israel could see that despite
her world reputation, Assyria didn't amount to much. Israel could
now attend to what was *really* going on. Nahum proclaimed,

GOD's *orders on Nineveh:*

"You're at the end of the line.
  It's all over with Nineveh.
I'm gutting your temple.
  Your gods and goddesses go in the trash.
I'm digging your grave. It's an unmarked grave.
  You're nothing — no, you're less than nothing!" . . .

"Assyria, I'm your enemy,"
  says GOD-*of-the-Angel-Armies.*
"I'll torch your chariots. They'll go up in smoke.
  'Lion Country' will be strewn with carcasses.

The war business is over — you're out of work:
    You'll have no more wars to report,
No more victories to announce.
    You're out of war work forever." (Nahum 1:14; 2:13)

Because Nahum has a single message — doom to Nineveh/
Assyria — it is easy to misunderstand the prophet as simply a
Nineveh-hater. But Nahum writes and preaches out of the large context in which Israel's sins are denounced as vigorously as those of
any of her enemies. The effect of Nahum is not to foment religious
hate against the enemy but to say, "Don't admire or be intimidated by
this enemy. They are going to be judged by the very same standards
applied to us."

HABAKKUK

Quick and Bold

Living by faith is a bewildering venture. We rarely know what's coming next, and not many things turn out the way we anticipate. It is natural to assume that since I am God's chosen and beloved, I will get favorable treatment from the God who favors me so extravagantly. It is not unreasonable to expect that from the time that I become his follower, I will be exempt from dead ends, muddy detours, and cruel treatment from the travelers I meet daily who are walking the other direction. That God-followers don't get preferential treatment in life always comes as a surprise. But it's also a surprise to find that there are a few men and women *within* the Bible who show up alongside us at such moments.

The prophet Habakkuk is one of them, and a most welcome companion he is. Most prophets, most of the time, speak God's Word *to us*. They are preachers calling us to listen to God's words of judgment and salvation, confrontation and comfort. They face us with God as he is, not as we imagine him to be. Most prophets are in-your-face assertive, not given to tact, not diplomatic, as they insist that we pay attention to God. But Habakkuk speaks our word *to God*. He gives voice to our bewilderment, articulates our puzzled attempts to make sense of things, faces God with our disappointment with God. He insists that God pay attention to us, and he insists with a prophet's characteristic no-nonsense bluntness.

> GOD, *how long do I have to cry out for help*
> *before you listen?*

How many times do I have to yell, "Help! Murder! Police!"
 before you come to the rescue?
Why do you force me to look at evil,
 stare trouble in the face day after day?
Anarchy and violence break out,
 quarrels and fights all over the place.
Law and order fall to pieces.
 Justice is a joke.
The wicked have the righteous hamstrung
 and stand justice on its head. (Habakkuk 1:1-4)

The circumstance that aroused Habakkuk took place in the seventh century B.C. The prophet realized that God was going to use the godless military machine of Babylon to bring God's judgment on God's own people — using a godless nation to punish a godly nation! It didn't make sense, and Habakkuk was quick and bold to say so. He dared to voice his feelings that God didn't know his own God business. Not a day has passed since then that one of us hasn't picked up and repeated Habakkuk's bafflement: "God, you don't seem to make sense!"

But this prophet companion who stands at our side does something even more important: He waits and he listens. It is in his waiting and listening — which then turns into his praying — that he found himself inhabiting the large world of God's sovereignty. Only there did he eventually realize that the believing-in-God life, the steady trusting-in-God life, is the full life, the only real life.

GOD, *I've heard what our ancestors say about you,*
 and I'm stopped in my tracks, down on my knees.
Do among us what you did among them.
 Work among us as you worked among them.

And as you bring judgment, as you surely must,
  remember mercy. . . .

Though the cherry trees don't blossom
  and the strawberries don't ripen,
Though the apples are worm-eaten
  and the wheat fields stunted,
Though the sheep pens are sheepless
  and the cattle barns empty,
I'm singing joyful praise to GOD.
  I'm turning cartwheels of joy to my Savior God.
Counting on GOD's *Rule to prevail,*
  I take heart and gain strength.
I run like a deer.
  I feel like I'm king of the mountain! (Habakkuk 3:1-2,17-19)

Habakkuk started out exactly where we start out with our puzzled complaints and God-accusations, but he didn't stay there. He ended up in a world, along with us, where every detail in our lives of love for God is worked into something good.

ZEPHANIAH

Seek God's Right Ways

We humans keep looking for a religion that will give us access to God without having to bother with people. We want to go to God for comfort and inspiration when we're fed up with the men and women and children around us. We want God to give us an edge in the dog-eat-dog competition of daily life.

This determination to get ourselves a religion that gives us an inside track with God, but leaves us free to deal with people however we like, is age-old. It is the sort of religion that has been promoted and marketed with both zeal and skill throughout human history. Business is always booming.

It is also the sort of religion that the biblical prophets are determined to root out. They are dead set against it. Through Zephaniah, God said,

> *"I'll find and punish those who are sitting it out, fat and lazy,*
> *amusing themselves and taking it easy,*
> *Who think, 'GOD doesn't do anything, good or bad.*
> *He isn't involved, so neither are we.'" (Zephaniah 1:12)*

Because the root of the solid spiritual life is embedded in a relationship between people and God, it is easy to develop the misunderstanding that my spiritual life is something personal between God and me — a private thing to be nurtured by prayers and singing, spiritual readings that comfort and inspire, and worship with like-minded friends. If we think this way for very long, we will assume that the way we treat the people we don't like or who don't like us has nothing to do with God.

That's when the prophets step in and interrupt us, insisting, "Everything you do or think or feel has to do with God. Every person you meet has to do with God." We live in a vast world of interconnectedness, and the connections have consequences, either in things or in people — and all the consequences come together in God. The biblical phrase for the coming together of the consequences is Judgment Day. In preparation for that day, Zephaniah implores his listeners,

> *Seek* GOD, *all you quietly disciplined people*
> *who live by* GOD's *justice.*
> *Seek* GOD's *right ways. Seek a quiet and disciplined life.*
> *Perhaps you'll be hidden on the Day of* GOD's *anger. (Zephaniah 2:3)*

We can't be reminded too often or too forcefully of this reckoning. Zephaniah's voice in the choir of prophets sustains the intensity, the urgency.

HAGGAI

Get to Work

Places of worship are a problem. And the problem does not seem to be architectural. Grand Gothic cathedrals that dominate a city don't ensure that the worship of God dominates that city. Unpainted, ramshackle, clapboard sheds perched precariously on the edge of a prairie don't guarantee a congregation of humble saints in denim.

As we look over the centuries of the many and various building projects in God's name — wilderness tabernacle, revival tent, Gothic cathedral, wayside chapel, synagogue, temple, meetinghouse, storefront mission, the catacombs — there doesn't seem to be any connection between the buildings themselves and the belief and behavior of the people who assemble in them.

In noticing this, it is not uncommon for us to be dismissive of the buildings themselves by saying, "A place of worship is not a building; it's people," or "I prefer worshiping God in the great cathedral of the outdoors." These pronouncements are often tagged with the scriptural punch line, "The God who made the universe doesn't live in custom-made shrines," which is supposed to end the discussion. God doesn't live in buildings — period. That's what we often say.

But then there is Haggai to account for. Haggai was dignified with the title "prophet" (therefore we must take him seriously), and, knowing God had sent Haggai, the governor and high priest "paid attention to him. In listening to Haggai, they honored GOD" (Haggai 1:12). His single task, carried out in a three-and-a-half-month mission, was to get God's people to work at rebuilding God's Temple (the same Temple that had been destroyed by God's decree only seventy or so years earlier). Haggai 2:1-5 says,

The Word of GOD *came through the prophet Haggai: "'. . . get to work,*
Zerubbabel!' — GOD *is speaking.*

"'Get to work, Joshua son of Jehozadak — high priest!'

"'Get to work, all you people!' — GOD *is speaking.*

"'Yes, get to work! For I am with you.' The GOD-*of-the-Angel-*
Armies is speaking! '. . . I'm living and breathing among you right now.
Don't be timid. Don't hold back.'"

Compared with the great prophets who preached repentance
and salvation, Haggai's message doesn't sound very "spiritual." But
in God's economy it is perhaps unwise to rank our assigned work
as either more or less spiritual. We are not angels; we inhabit space.
Material — bricks and mortar, boards and nails — keeps us grounded
and connected with the ordinary world in which we necessarily live
out our extraordinary beliefs. Haggai keeps us in touch with those
times in our lives when repairing the building where we worship is
an act of obedience every bit as important as praying in that place of
worship.

ZECHARIAH

Working Together

Zechariah shared with his contemporary Haggai the prophetic task of getting the people of Judah to rebuild their ruined Temple. Their preaching pulled the people out of self-preoccupation and got them working together as a people of God. There was a job to do, and the two prophets teamed up to make sure it got done.

But Zechariah did more than that. For the people were faced with more than a ruined Temple and city. Their self-identity as the people of God was in ruins. For a century they had been knocked around by the world powers, kicked and mocked, used and abused. This once-proud people, their glorious sacred history starred with the names of Abraham, Moses, Samuel, David, and Isaiah, had been treated with contempt for so long that they were in danger of losing all connection with that past, losing their magnificent identity as God's people.

Zechariah was a major factor in recovering the magnificence from the ruins of a degrading exile. Zechariah reinvigorated their imaginations with his visions and messages. The visions provided images of a sovereign God that worked their way into the lives of the people, countering the long ordeal of debasement and ridicule.

A Message from GOD-of-the-Angel-Armies:
"In the same way that I decided to punish you when your ancestors made me angry, and didn't pull my punches, at this time I've decided to bless Jerusalem and the country of Judah. Don't be afraid. And now here's what I want you to do: Tell the truth, the whole truth, when you speak. Do the right thing by one another, both personally and in your courts. Don't cook up plans to take unfair advantage of others. Don't

*do or say what isn't so. I hate all that stuff. Keep your lives simple and
honest." Decree of GOD. (Zechariah 8:14-17)*

The messages forged a fresh vocabulary that gave energy and
credibility to the long-term purposes of God being worked out in their
lives.

*GOD-of-the-Angel-Armies will step in
    and take care of his flock, the people of Judah.
He'll revive their spirits,
    make them proud to be on God's side.
God will use them in his work of rebuilding,
    use them as foundations and pillars,
Use them as tools and instruments
    use them to oversee his work.
They'll be a workforce to be proud of, working as one,
    their heads held high, striding through swamps and mud,
Courageous and vigorous because GOD is with them,
    undeterred by the world's thugs. (Zechariah 10:3-5)*

But that isn't the end of it. Zechariah's enigmatic visions, working at multiple levels, and his poetically charged messages are at work
still, like time capsules in the lives of God's people, continuing to
release insight and hope and clarity for the people whom God is using
to work out his purposes in a world that has no language for God and
the purposes of God.

*What a Day that will be! No more cold nights — in fact, no more
nights! The Day is coming — the timing is GOD's — when it will be*

continuous day. Every evening will be a fresh morning.

What a Day that will be! Fresh flowing rivers out of Jerusalem, half to the eastern sea, half to the western sea, flowing year-round, summer and winter!

GOD will be king over all the earth, one GOD and only one. What a Day that will be! (Zechariah 14:6-9)

MALACHI

The Last Word

Most of life is not lived in crisis — which is a good thing. Not many of us would be able to sustain a life of perpetual pain or loss or ecstasy or challenge. But crisis has this to say for it: In time of crisis everything, absolutely everything, is important and significant. Life itself is on the line. No word is casual, no action marginal. And almost always, God and our relationship with God is on the front page.

But during the humdrum times, when things are, as we tend to say, "normal," our interest in God is crowded to the margins of our lives and we become preoccupied with ourselves. "Religion" during such times is trivialized into asking "God-questions" — calling God into question or complaining about him, treating the worship of God as a mere hobby or diversion, managing our personal affairs (such as marriage) for our own convenience and disregarding what God has to say about them, going about our usual activities as if God were not involved in such dailiness.

The prophecy of Malachi is made to order for just such conditions. Malachi creates a crisis at a time when we are unaware of crisis. He wakes us up to the crisis of God during the times when the only thing we are concerned with is us. He keeps us on our toes, listening for God, waiting in anticipation for God, ready to respond to God, who is always coming to us.

GOD *says, "You have spoken hard, rude words to me.*

"You ask, 'When did we ever do that?'

"When you said, 'It doesn't pay to serve God. What do we ever get out of it? When we did what he said and went around with long faces,

serious about GOD-of-the-Angel-Armies, what difference did it make?
Those who take life into their own hands are the lucky ones. They break
all the rules and get ahead anyway. They push God to the limit and get
by with it.'"

Then those whose lives honored GOD got together and talked it over.
GOD saw what they were doing and listened in. A book was opened in
God's presence and minutes were taken of the meeting, with the names
of the GOD-fearers written down, all the names of those who honored
GOD's name.

GOD-of-the-Angel-Armies said, "They're mine, all mine. They'll
get special treatment when I go into action. I treat them with the same
consideration and kindness that parents give the child who honors them.
Once more you'll see the difference it makes between being a person who
does the right thing and one who doesn't, between serving God and not
serving him." (Malachi 3:13-18)

Malachi gets in the last word of Holy Scripture in the Old
Testament. The final sentences in his message to us evoke the gigantic
figures of Moses and Elijah — Moses to keep us rooted in what God
has done and said in the past, Elijah to keep us alert to what God will
do in the days ahead.

"Remember and keep the revelation I gave through my servant Moses,
the revelation I commanded at Horeb for all Israel, all the rules and
procedures for right living.

"But also look ahead: I'm sending Elijah the prophet to clear the
way for the Big Day of GOD — the decisive Judgment Day! He will
convince parents to look after their children and children to look up to
their parents. If they refuse, I'll come and put the land under a curse."
(Malachi 4:4-6)

By leaving us in the company of mighty Moses and fiery Elijah, Malachi considerably reduces the danger of our trivializing matters of God and the soul.

THE NEW TESTAMENT

THE NEW TESTAMENT

THE BEGINNING OF A NEW ERA

The arrival of Jesus signaled the beginning of a new era. God entered history in a personal way, and made it unmistakably clear that he is on our side, doing everything possible to save us. It was all presented and worked out in the life, death, and resurrection of Jesus. It was, and is, hard to believe — seemingly too good to be true. One of Jesus' disciples, John, summed it up in the introduction of his first letter:

> From the very first day, we were there, taking it all in — we heard it with our own ears, saw it with our own eyes, verified it with our own hands. The Word of Life appeared right before our eyes; we saw it happen! And now we're telling you in most sober prose that what we witnessed was, incredibly, this: The infinite Life of God himself took shape before us.
>
> We saw it, we heard it, and now we're telling you so you can experience it along with us, this experience of communion with the Father and his Son, Jesus Christ. Our motive for writing is simply this: We want you to enjoy this, too. Your joy will double our joy! (1 John 1:1-4)

But one by one, men and women did believe it, believed Jesus was God alive among them and for them. Soon they would realize that he also lived in them. To their great surprise they found themselves living in a world where God called all the shots — had the first word on everything; had the last word on everything. In fact, in John's vision, he heard Jesus say, "I'm A to Z, the First and the Final, Beginning and Conclusion" (Revelation 22:13). That meant that everything, quite literally every thing, had to be re-centered, re-imagined, and re-thought.

They went at it with immense gusto. They told stories of Jesus and arranged his teachings in memorable form. They wrote letters. They sang songs. They prayed. One of them wrote an extraordinary poem based on holy visions. There was no apparent organization to any of this; it was all more or less spontaneous and, to the eye of the casual observer, haphazard. Over the course of about fifty years, these writings added up to what would later be compiled by the followers of Jesus and designated "The New Testament."

Three kinds of writing — eyewitness stories, personal letters, and a visionary poem — make up the book. Five stories, twenty-one letters, one poem.

In the course of this writing and reading, collecting and arranging, with no one apparently in charge, the early Christians, whose lives were being changed and shaped by what they were reading, arrived at the conviction that there was, in fact, someone in charge — God's Holy Spirit was behind and in it all. In retrospect, they could see that it was not at all random or haphazard, that every word worked with every other word, and that all the separate documents worked in intricate harmony. There was nothing accidental in any of this, nothing merely circumstantial. They were bold to call what had been written "God's Word," and trusted their lives to it. They accepted its authority over their lives. In his second letter to his protégé Timothy, Paul wrote,

There's nothing like the written Word of God for showing you the way
to salvation through faith in Christ Jesus. Every part of Scripture is
God-breathed and useful one way or another — showing us truth, expos-
ing our rebellion, correcting our mistakes, training us to live God's way.
Through the Word we are put together and shaped up for the tasks God
has for us. (2 Timothy 3:15-17)

Most of its readers since have been similarly convinced.

A striking feature in all this writing is that it was done in the street language of the day, the idiom of the playground and marketplace. In the Greek-speaking world of that day, there were two levels of language: formal and informal. Formal language was used to write philosophy and history, government decrees and epic poetry. If someone were to sit down and consciously write for posterity, it would of course be written in this formal language with its learned vocabulary and precise diction. But if the writing was routine — shopping lists, family letters, bills, and receipts — it was written in the common, informal idiom of everyday speech, street language.

And this is the language used throughout the New Testament. Some people are taken aback by this, supposing that language dealing with a holy God and holy things should be elevated — stately and ceremonial. But one good look at Jesus — his preference for down-to-earth stories and easy association with common people — gets rid of that supposition. For Jesus is the descent of God to our lives, just as they are, not the ascent of our lives to God, hoping he might approve when he sees how hard we try. No, Jesus became one of us, moving, as John said, "into the neighborhood" (John 1:14). And Paul wrote,

He had equal status with God but didn't think so much of himself that
he had to cling to the advantages of that status no matter what. Not at
all. When the time came, he set aside the privileges of deity and took on

the status of a slave, became human! *Having become human, he stayed
human. It was an incredibly humbling process. He didn't claim special
privileges. Instead, he lived a selfless, obedient life and then died a selfless, obedient death.* (Philippians 2:5-8)

And that is why the followers of Jesus in their witness and preaching, translating and teaching, have always done their best to get the
Message — the "good news" — into the language of whatever streets
they happen to be living on. In order to understand the Message right,
the language must be right — not a refined language that appeals to
our aspirations after the best but a rough and earthy language that
reveals God's presence and action where we least expect it, catching
us when we are up to our elbows in the soiled ordinariness of our lives
and God is the furthest thing from our minds.

This version of the New Testament in a contemporary idiom keeps
the language of the Message current and fresh and understandable in
the same language in which we do our shopping, talk with our friends,
worry about world affairs, and teach our children their table manners.
The goal is not to render a word-for-word conversion of Greek into
English, but rather to convert the tone, the rhythm, the events, the
ideas, into the way we actually think and speak.

In the midst of doing this work, I realized that this is exactly
what I have been doing all my vocational life. For thirty-five years as a
pastor I stood at the border between two languages, biblical Greek and
everyday English, acting as a translator, providing the right phrases,
getting the right words so that the men and women to whom I was
pastor could find their way around and get along in this world where
God has spoken so decisively and clearly in Jesus. I did it from the
pulpit and in the kitchen, in hospitals and restaurants, in parking lots
and at picnics, always looking for an English way to make the biblical
text relevant to the conditions of the people.

THE MEDITERRANEAN SEA

Sidon

ITUREA
Damascus
SYRIA

Mount Hermon

Tyre
Caesarea-Philippi

PHOENICIA

GALILEE
Hazor
Chorazin
Capernaum
Ptolemais
Gennesaret
Cana
Magdala
Nazareth
Tiberias
Nain

Bethsaida
Gergesa

GAULANITIS
TETRARCHY OF PHILIP

TRACHONITIS
Raphana

Sea of Galilee
Hippos

BATANEA

Gadara
Abila

AURANITIS

Dor
Megiddo
Caesarea
Dothan

SAMARIA

Scythopolis

Pella

Dion

Sebaste

Amataus

Gerasa

Sychar

Antipatris
Alexandrium

PEREA

DECAPOLIS

Joppa
Lydda
Bethel
Ephraim
Aijalon
Jamnia
Jericho
Emmaus
Cyprus
Jerusalem
Bethany
Hyncania
Bethlehem
Herodium
Azotus

Jordan River

Philadelphia

Esbus
Medeba

Ashkelon
JUDEA
Hebron
Adora
Gaza

Machaerus

Dead Sea

Engedi

Raphia
IDUMEA
Arad
Masada
Beersheba
Malatha

NABATEA

PALESTINE IN THE TIME OF JESUS

0   10   20   30 mi.

0 10 20 30 40   km.

MATTHEW

Fulfilled

The story of Jesus doesn't begin with Jesus. God had been at work for a long time. Salvation, which is the main business of Jesus, is an old business. Jesus is the coming together in final form of themes and energies and movements that had been set in motion before the foundation of the world.

Matthew opens the New Testament by setting the local story of Jesus in its world historical context. He makes sure that as we read his account of the birth, life, death, and resurrection of Jesus, we see the connections with everything that has gone before. In fact, in his account of Jesus' birth alone, Matthew reminds his readers of two Old Testament prophecies being fulfilled in the coming of the Messiah.

Watch for this — a virgin will get pregnant and bear a son; they will name him Immanuel (Hebrew for "God is with us"). (Matthew 1:23, quoting Isaiah 7:14)

It's you, Bethlehem, in Judah's land, no longer bringing up the rear. From you will come the leader who will shepherd-rule my people, my Israel. (Matthew 2:5-6, quoting Micah 5:2)

"Fulfilled" is one of Matthew's characteristic verbs: such and such happened "that it might be *fulfilled*." Jesus is unique, but he is not odd.

Better yet, Matthew tells the story in such a way that not only is everything previous to us completed in Jesus; we are completed in

Jesus. Every day we wake up in the middle of something that is already going on, that has been going on for a long time: genealogy and geology, history and culture, the cosmos — God. We are neither accidental nor incidental to the story. We get orientation, briefing, background, reassurance.

Matthew provides the comprehensive context by which we see all God's creation and salvation completed in Jesus, and all the parts of our lives — work, family, friends, memories, dreams — also completed in Jesus, who himself said, "Don't suppose for a minute that I have come to demolish the Scriptures — either God's Law or the Prophets. I'm not here to demolish but to complete. I am going to put it all together, pull it all together in a vast panorama" (Matthew 5:17). Lacking such a context, we are in danger of seeing Jesus as a mere diversion from the concerns announced in the newspapers. Nothing could be further from the truth.

MARK

God Is Passionate to Save Us

Mark wastes no time in getting down to business — a single-sentence introduction ("The good news of Jesus Christ — the Message! — begins here"), and not a digression to be found from beginning to end. An event has taken place that radically changes the way we look at and experience the world, and he can't wait to tell us about it. There's an air of breathless excitement in nearly every sentence he writes. The sooner we get the message, the better off we'll be, for the message is good, incredibly good: God is here, and he's on our side. Mark says he even calls us "family."

> *He was surrounded by the crowd when he was given the message, "Your mother and brothers and sisters are outside looking for you."*
>
> *Jesus responded, "Who do you think are my mother and brothers?" Looking around, taking in everyone seated around him, he said, "Right here, right in front of you — my mother and my brothers. Obedience is thicker than blood. The person who obeys God's will is my brother and sister and mother." (Mark 3:32-35)*

The bare announcement that God exists doesn't particularly qualify as news. Most people in most centuries have believed in the existence of God or gods. It may well be, in fact, that human beings in aggregate and through the centuries have given more attention and concern to divinity than to all their other concerns put together — food, housing, clothing, pleasure, work, family, whatever.

But that God is here right now, and on our side, actively seeking to help us in the way we most need help — *this* qualifies as news. For, common as belief in God is, there is also an enormous amount of guesswork and gossip surrounding the subject, which results in runaway superstition, anxiety, and exploitation. So Mark, understandably, is in a hurry to tell us what happened in the birth, life, death, and resurrection of Jesus — the Event that reveals the truth of God to us, so that we can live in reality and not illusion. He doesn't want us to waste a minute of these precious lives of ours ignorant of this most practical of all matters — that God is passionate to save us.

LUKE

There Are No Outsiders

Most of us, most of the time, feel left out — misfits. We don't belong. Others seem to be so confident, so sure of themselves, "insiders" who know the ropes, old hands in a club from which we are excluded.

One of the ways we have of responding to this is to form our own club, or join one that will have us. Here is at least one place where we are "in" and the others "out." The clubs range from informal to formal in gatherings that are variously political, social, cultural, and economic. But the one thing they have in common is the principle of exclusion. Identity or worth is achieved by excluding all but the chosen. The terrible price we pay for keeping all those other people out so that we can savor the sweetness of being insiders is a reduction of reality, a shrinkage of life.

Nowhere is this price more terrible than when it is paid in the cause of religion. But religion has a long history of doing just that, of reducing the huge mysteries of God to the respectability of club rules, of shrinking the vast human community to a "membership." But with God there are no outsiders. Jesus said, "The Son of Man came to find and restore the lost" (Luke 19:10).

Luke is a most vigorous champion of the outsider. An outsider himself, the only Gentile in an all-Jewish cast of New Testament writers, he shows how Jesus includes those who typically were treated as outsiders by the religious establishment of the day: women, common laborers (sheepherders), the racially different (Samaritans), the poor. He will not countenance religion as a club. As Luke tells the story, all of us who have found ourselves on the outside looking in on life with no hope of gaining entrance (and who of us hasn't felt it?) now find the doors wide open, found and welcomed by God in Jesus, who, in fact said, "Ask and you'll get; seek and you'll find; knock and the door will open" (Luke 11:9).

JOHN

Putting It All Together

In Genesis, the first book of the Bible, God is presented as speaking the creation into existence. God speaks the word and it happens: heaven and earth, ocean and stream, trees and grass, birds and fish, animals and humans. Everything, seen and unseen, called into being by God's spoken word.

In deliberate parallel to the opening words of Genesis, John presents God as speaking salvation into existence. "The Word was first, the Word present to God, God present to the Word. The Word was God, in readiness for God from day one" (John 1:1-2). This time God's word takes on human form and enters history in the person of Jesus. Jesus speaks the word and it happens: forgiveness and judgment, healing and illumination, mercy and grace, joy and love, freedom and resurrection. Everything broken and fallen, sinful and diseased, called into salvation by God's spoken word.

For, somewhere along the line things went wrong (Genesis tells that story, too) and are in desperate need of fixing. The fixing is all accomplished by speaking — God speaking salvation into being in the person of Jesus. Jesus, in this account, not only speaks the word of God; he *is* the Word of God.

Keeping company with these words, we begin to realize that our words are more important than we ever supposed. Saying "I believe," for instance, marks the difference between life and death. John wrote, "Jesus provided far more God-revealing signs than are written down in this book. These are written down so you will believe that Jesus is the Messiah, the Son of God, and in the act of believing, have real and eternal life in the way he personally revealed it" (John 20:30-31). Our words accrue dignity and gravity in conversations with Jesus.

For Jesus doesn't impose salvation as a solution; he *narrates* salvation into being through leisurely conversation, intimate personal relationships, compassionate responses, passionate prayer, and — putting it all together — a sacrificial death. We don't casually walk away from words like that.

ACTS

In on the Action

Because the story of Jesus is so impressive — God among us! God speaking a language we can understand! God acting in ways that heal and help and save us! — there is a danger that we will be impressed, but only be impressed. As the spectacular dimensions of this story slowly (or suddenly) dawn upon us, we could easily become enthusiastic spectators, and then let it go at that — become admirers of Jesus, generous with our oohs and ahs, and in our better moments inspired to imitate him.

It is Luke's task to prevent that, to prevent us from becoming mere spectators to Jesus, fans of the Message. Of the original quartet of writers on Jesus, Luke alone continues to tell the story as the apostles and disciples live it into the next generation. The remarkable thing is that it continues to be essentially the same story. Luke continues his narration with hardly a break, a pause perhaps to dip his pen in the inkwell, writing in the same style, using the same vocabulary.

The story of Jesus doesn't end with Jesus. It continues in the lives of those who believe in him. The supernatural does not stop with Jesus. He told his disciples, "You'll get . . . the Holy Spirit. And when the Holy Spirit comes on you, you will be able to be my witnesses in Jerusalem, all over Judea and Samaria, even to the ends of the world" (Acts 1:8). And about midway through the book, we read, "This Message of salvation spread like wildfire all through the region" (Acts 13:49). Luke makes it clear that these Christians he wrote about were no more spectators of Jesus than Jesus was a spectator of God — they are *in* on the action of God, God acting *in* them, God living *in* them. Which also means, of course, in *us*.

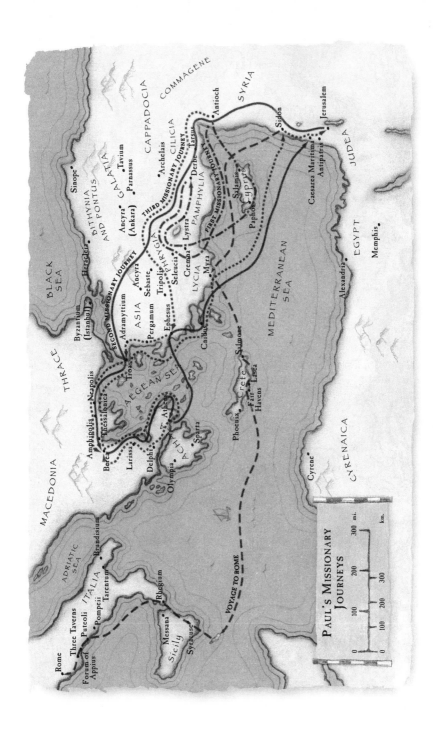

PAUL'S MISSIONARY JOURNEYS

ROMANS

Exuberant and Passionate Thinking

The event that split history into "before" and "after" and changed the world took place about thirty years before Paul wrote this letter. The event — the life, death, and resurrection of Jesus — took place in a remote corner of the extensive Roman Empire: the province of Judea in Palestine. Hardly anyone noticed, certainly no one in busy and powerful Rome.

And when this letter arrived in Rome, hardly anyone read it, certainly no one of influence. There was much to read in Rome — imperial decrees, exquisite poetry, finely crafted moral philosophy — and much of it was world-class. And yet in no time, as such things go, this letter left all those other writings in the dust. Paul's letter to the Romans has had a far larger impact on its readers than the volumes of all those Roman writers put together.

The quick rise of this letter to a peak of influence is extraordinary, written as it was by an obscure Roman citizen without connections. But when we read it for ourselves, we begin to realize that it is the letter itself that is truly extraordinary, and that no obscurity in writer or readers could have kept it obscure for long.

The letter to the Romans is a piece of exuberant and passionate thinking. This is the glorious life of the mind enlisted in the service of God. Paul takes the well-witnessed and devoutly believed fact of the life, death, and resurrection of Jesus of Nazareth and thinks through its implications. How does it happen that in the death and resurrection of Jesus, world history took a new direction, and at the same moment the life of every man, woman, and child on the planet was eternally affected? Paul responded,

*Those who enter into Christ's being-here-for-us no longer have to live
under a continuous, low-lying black cloud. A new power is in operation.
The Spirit of life in Christ, like a strong wind, has magnificently cleared
the air, freeing you from a fated lifetime of brutal tyranny at the hands
of sin and death. (Romans 8:1-2)*

What is God up to? Paul asks a few more questions before he gets
to the answer.

*Is there anyone around who can explain God?
Anyone smart enough to tell him what to do?
Anyone who has done him such a huge favor
      that God has to ask his advice?*

*Everything comes from him;
Everything happens through him;
Everything ends up in him.
Always glory! Always praise! (Romans 11:34-36)*

What does it *mean* that Jesus "saves"?

*He presented himself for this sacrificial death when we were far too
weak and rebellious to do anything to get ourselves ready. And even if
we hadn't been so weak, we wouldn't have known what to do anyway.
We can understand someone dying for a person worth dying for, and we
can understand how someone good and noble could inspire us to selfless
sacrifice. But God put his love on the line for us by offering his Son in
sacrificial death while we were of no use whatever to him.
      Now that we are set right with God by means of this sacrificial*

death, the consummate blood sacrifice, there is no longer a question of being at odds with God in any way. If, when we were at our worst, we were put on friendly terms with God by the sacrificial death of his Son, now that we're at our best, just think of how our lives will expand and deepen by means of his resurrection life! (Romans 5:6-10)

What's behind all this, and where is it going?

God knew what he was doing from the very beginning. He decided from the outset to shape the lives of those who love him along the same lines as the life of his Son. The Son stands first in the line of humanity he restored. We see the original and intended shape of our lives there in him. After God made that decision of what his children should be like, he followed it up by calling people by name. After he called them by name, he set them on a solid basis with himself. And then, after getting them established, he stayed with them to the end, gloriously completing what he had begun. (Romans 8:29-30)

These are the questions — and a brief look at the answers — that drive Paul's thinking. Paul's mind is supple and capacious. He takes logic and argument, poetry and imagination, Scripture and prayer, creation and history and experience, and weaves them into this letter that has become the premier document of Christian theology.

1 Corinthians

Message of the "Good News"

When people become Christians, they don't at the same moment become nice. This always comes as something of a surprise. Conversion to Christ and his ways doesn't automatically furnish a person with impeccable manners and suitable morals.

The people of Corinth had a reputation in the ancient world as an unruly, hard-drinking, sexually promiscuous bunch of people. When Paul arrived with the Message and many of them became believers in Jesus, they brought their reputations with them right into the church.

Paul spent a year and a half with them as their pastor, going over the Message of the "good news" in detail, showing them how to live out this new life of salvation and holiness as a community of believers. Then he went on his way to other towns and churches.

Sometime later Paul received a report from one of the Corinthian families that in his absence things had more or less fallen apart. He also received a letter from Corinth asking for help. Factions had developed, morals were in disrepair, worship had degenerated into a selfish grabbing for the supernatural. It was the kind of thing that might have been expected from Corinthians!

Paul's first letter to the Corinthians is a classic of pastoral response: affectionate, firm, clear, and unswerving in the conviction that God among them, revealed in Jesus and present in his Holy Spirit, continued to be the central issue in their lives, regardless of how much of a mess they had made of things.

Don't you realize that this is not the way to live? Unjust people who don't care about God will not be joining in his kingdom. Those who use and abuse each other, use and abuse sex, use and abuse the earth and everything in it, don't qualify as citizens in God's kingdom. A number of you know from experience what I'm talking about, for not so long ago you were on that list. Since then, you've been cleaned up and given a fresh start by Jesus, our Master, our Messiah, and by our God present in us, the Spirit.

Just because something is technically legal doesn't mean that it's spiritually appropriate. (1 Corinthians 6:9-12)

Paul doesn't disown them as brother and sister Christians, doesn't throw them out because of their bad behavior, and doesn't fly into a tirade over their irresponsible ways. He takes it all more or less in stride, but also takes them by the hand and goes over all the old ground again, directing them in how to work all the glorious details of God's saving love into their love for one another.

Love never dies. Inspired speech will be over some day; praying in tongues will end; understanding will reach its limit. We know only a portion of the truth, and what we say about God is always incomplete. But when the Complete arrives, our incompletes will be canceled. . . .

But for right now, until that completeness, we have three things to do to lead us toward that consummation: Trust steadily in God, hope unswervingly, love extravagantly. And the best of the three is love.

Go after a life of love as if your life depended on it — because it does. (1 Corinthians 13:8-10,13; 14:1)

2 CORINTHIANS

Profound and Vigorous Writing

The Corinthian Christians gave their founding pastor, Paul, more trouble than all his other churches put together. No sooner did Paul get one problem straightened out in Corinth than three more appeared.

For anyone operating under the naive presumption that joining a Christian church is a good way to meet all the best people and cultivate smooth social relations, a reading of Paul's Corinthian correspondence is the prescribed cure. But however much trouble the Corinthians were to each other and to Paul, they prove to be a cornucopia of blessings to us, for they triggered some of Paul's most profound and vigorous writing.

The provocation for Paul's second letter to the Christians in Corinth was an attack on his leadership. In his first letter, though he wrote most kindly and sympathetically, he didn't mince words. He wrote with the confident authority of a pastor who understands the ways God's salvation works and the kind of community that comes into being as a result. At least some of what he wrote to them was hard to hear and hard to take.

So they bucked his authority—accused him of inconsistencies, impugned his motives, questioned his credentials. They didn't argue with what he had written; they simply denied his right to tell them what to do.

And so Paul was forced to defend his leadership.

If you're looking for a clear example of someone on Christ's side, why do you so quickly cut me out? Believe me, I am quite sure of my standing with Christ. You may think I overstate the authority he gave me, but I'm not backing off. Every bit of my commitment is for the purpose of building you up, after all, not tearing you down. . . . We aren't making outrageous claims here. We're sticking to the limits of what God has set for us. But there can be no question that those limits reach to and include you. . . . What we're hoping for is that as your lives grow in faith, you'll play a part within our expanding work. (2 Corinthians 10:7-8,13,15)

After mopping up a few details left over from the first letter, he confronted the challenge, and in the process probed the very nature of leadership in a community of believers. For example, Paul wanted to be "partners" with the Corinthians, "working alongside" them, "joyfully expectant" (2 Corinthians 1:24). And he knew "cheerfully pleasing God is the main thing" (2 Corinthians 5:9).

Because leadership is necessarily an exercise of authority, it easily shifts into an exercise of power. But the minute it does that, it begins to inflict damage on both the leader and the led. Paul, studying Jesus, had learned a kind of leadership in which he managed to stay out of the way so that the others could deal with God without having to go through him. He saw himself as an ambassador.

We're Christ's representatives. God uses us to persuade men and women to drop their differences and enter into God's work of making things right between them. We're speaking for Christ himself now: Become friends with God; he's already a friend with you. (2 Corinthians 5:20)

All who are called to exercise leadership in whatever capacity — parent or coach, pastor or president, teacher or manager — can be grateful to Paul for this letter, and to the Corinthians for provoking it.

GALATIANS

Free from Within

When men and women get their hands on religion, one of the first things they often do is turn it into an instrument for controlling others, either putting or keeping them "in their place." The history of such religious manipulation and coercion is long and tedious. It is little wonder that people who have only known religion on such terms experience release or escape from it as freedom. The problem is that the freedom turns out to be short-lived.

Paul of Tarsus was doing his diligent best to add yet another chapter to this dreary history when he was converted by Jesus to something radically and entirely different — a free life in God. Through Jesus, Paul learned that God was not an impersonal force to be used to make people behave in certain prescribed ways, but a personal Savior who set us free to live a free life. God did not coerce us from without, but set us free from within.

It was a glorious experience, and Paul set off telling others, introducing and inviting everyone he met into this free life. In his early travels he founded a series of churches in the Roman province of Galatia. A few years later Paul learned that religious leaders of the old school had come into those churches, called his views and authority into question, and were reintroducing the old ways, herding all these freedom-loving Christians back into the corral of religious rules and regulations.

Paul was, of course, furious. He was furious with the old guard for coming in with their strong-arm religious tactics and intimidating the Christians into giving up their free life in Jesus. But he was also furious with the Christians for caving in to the intimidation, and he had no qualms about speaking his mind.

*Are you going to continue this craziness? For only crazy people would
think they could complete by their own efforts what was begun by God.
If you weren't smart enough or strong enough to begin it, how do you
suppose you could perfect it? Did you go through this whole painful
learning process for nothing? It is not yet a total loss, but it certainly will
be if you keep this up!* (Galatians 3:2-4)

His letter to the Galatian churches helps them, and us, recover the
original freedom.

*My counsel is this: Live freely, animated and motivated by God's Spirit.
Then you won't feed the compulsions of selfishness. For there is a root of
sinful self-interest in us that is at odds with a free spirit, just as the free
spirit is incompatible with selfishness. These two ways of life are anti-
thetical, so that you cannot live at times one way and at times another
way according to how you feel on any given day. Why don't you choose to
be led by the Spirit and so escape the erratic compulsions of a law-
dominated existence?* (Galatians 5:16-18)

It also gives direction in the nature of God's gift of freedom — most
necessary guidance, for freedom is a delicate and subtle gift, easily
perverted and often squandered.

EPHESIANS

An Exuberant Exploration

What we know about God and what we do for God have a way of getting broken apart in our lives. The moment the organic unity of belief and behavior is damaged in any way, we are incapable of living out the full humanity for which we were created.

Paul's letter to the Ephesians joins together what has been torn apart in our sin-wrecked world. He begins with an exuberant exploration of what Christians believe about God, and then, like a surgeon skillfully setting a compound fracture, "sets" this belief in God into our behavior before God so that the bones — belief and behavior — knit together and heal. He knew, however, that his surgical skills were limited, so he not only wrote; he prayed, asking

> *The God of our Master, Jesus Christ, the God of glory — to make you intelligent and discerning in knowing him personally, your eyes focused and clear, so that you can see exactly what it is he is calling you to do, grasp the immensity of this glorious way of life he has for his followers, oh, the utter extravagance of his work in us who trust him — endless energy, boundless strength! (Ephesians 1:17-19)*

Once our attention is called to it, we notice these fractures all over the place. There is hardly a bone in our bodies that has escaped injury, hardly a relationship in city or job, school or church, family or country, that isn't out of joint or limping in pain. There is much work to be done.

And so Paul goes to work. He ranges widely, from heaven to earth

and back again, showing how Jesus, the Messiah, is eternally and tire-
lessly bringing everything and everyone together.

> *Christ brought us together through his death on the cross. The Cross got*
> *us to embrace, and that was the end of the hostility. Christ came and*
> *preached peace to you outsiders and peace to us insiders. He treated us*
> *as equals, and so made us equals. Through him we both share the same*
> *Spirit and have equal access to the Father. . . . You were all called to*
> *travel on the same road and in the same direction, so stay together, both*
> *outwardly and inwardly. You have one Master, one faith, one baptism,*
> *one God and Father of all, who rules over all, works through all, and is*
> *present in all. Everything you are and think and do is permeated with*
> *Oneness. (Ephesians 2:16-18; 4:4-6)*

He also shows us that in addition to having this work done in and
for us, we are participants in this most urgent work.

> *Get out there and walk — better yet, run! — on the road God called you*
> *to travel. I don't want any of you sitting around on your hands. I don't*
> *want anyone strolling off, down some path that goes nowhere. And mark*
> *that you do this with humility and discipline — not in fits and starts,*
> *but steadily, pouring yourselves out for each other in acts of love, alert at*
> *noticing differences and quick at mending fences. (Ephesians 4:1-3)*

Now that we know what is going on, that the energy of reconcili-
ation is the dynamo at the heart of the universe, it is imperative that
we join in vigorously and perseveringly, convinced that every detail
in our lives contributes (or not) to what Paul describes as God's plan

worked out by Christ, "a long-range plan in which everything would be brought together and summed up in him, everything in deepest heaven, everything on planet earth."

PHILIPPIANS

Spilling Out

This is Paul's happiest letter. And the happiness is infectious. Before we've read a dozen lines, we begin to feel the joy ourselves — the dance of words and the exclamations of delight have a way of getting inside us.

But happiness is not a word we can understand by looking it up in the dictionary. In fact, none of the qualities of the Christian life can be learned out of a book. Something more like apprenticeship is required, being around someone who out of years of devoted discipline shows us, by his or her entire behavior, what it is. Moments of verbal instruction will certainly occur, but mostly an apprentice acquires skill by daily and intimate association with a "master," picking up subtle but absolutely essential things, such as timing and rhythm and "touch."

When we read what Paul wrote to the Christian believers in the city of Philippi, we find ourselves in the company of just such a master. Paul doesn't tell us that we can be happy, or how to be happy. He simply and unmistakably *is* happy. None of his circumstances contribute to his joy: He wrote from a jail cell, his work was under attack by competitors, and after twenty years or so of hard traveling in the service of Jesus, he was tired and would have welcomed some relief.

But circumstances are incidental compared to the life of Jesus, the Messiah, that Paul experiences from the inside. For it is a life that not only happened at a certain point in history, but continues to happen, spilling out into the lives of those who receive him, and then continues to spill out all over the place. Here's how Paul envisioned his readers spilling out the life of Christ:

Do everything readily and cheerfully — no bickering, no second-guessing allowed! Go out into the world uncorrupted, a breath of fresh air in this squalid and polluted society. Provide people with a glimpse of good living and of the living God. Carry the light-giving Message into the night. (Philippians 2:14-15)

Christ is, among much else, the revelation that God cannot be contained or hoarded.

So this is my prayer: that your love will flourish and that you will not only love much but well. Learn to love appropriately. You need to use your head and test your feelings so that your love is sincere and intelligent, not sentimental gush. Live a lover's life, circumspect and exemplary, a life Jesus will be proud of: bountiful in fruits from the soul, making Jesus Christ attractive to all, getting everyone involved in the glory and praise of God. (Philippians 1:9-11)

It is this "spilling out" quality of Christ's life that accounts for the happiness of Christians, for joy is life in excess, the overflow of what cannot be contained within any one person.

COLOSSIANS

A Most Remarkable Greatness

Hardly anyone who hears the full story of Jesus and learns the true facts of his life and teaching, crucifixion and resurrection, walks away with a shrug of the shoulders, dismissing him as unimportant. People ignorant of the story or misinformed about it, of course, regularly dismiss him. But with few exceptions, the others know instinctively that they are dealing with a most remarkable greatness.

But it is quite common for those who consider him truly important to include others who seem to be equally important in his company — Buddha, Moses, Socrates, and Muhammad for a historical start, along with some personal favorites. For these people, Jesus is important, but not central; his prestige is considerable, but he is not preeminent.

The Christians in the town of Colosse, or at least some of them, seem to have been taking this line. For them, cosmic forces of one sort or another were getting equal billing with Jesus. Paul writes to them in an attempt to restore Jesus, the Messiah, to the center of their lives.

Watch out for people who try to dazzle you with big words and intellectual double-talk. They want to drag you off into endless arguments that never amount to anything. They spread their ideas through the empty traditions of human beings and the empty superstitions of spirit beings. But that's not the way of Christ. Everything of God gets expressed in him, so you can see and hear him clearly. You don't need a telescope, a microscope, or a horoscope to realize the fullness of Christ, and the emptiness of the universe without him. When you come to him, that fullness comes together for you, too. His power extends over everything. (Colossians 2:8-10)

The way he makes his argument is as significant as the argument he makes. Claims for the uniqueness of Jesus are common enough. But such claims about Jesus are frequently made with an arrogance that is completely incompatible with Jesus himself. Sometimes the claims are enforced with violence.

But Paul, although unswervingly confident in the conviction that Christ occupies the center of creation and salvation without peers, is not arrogant. And he is certainly not violent. He argues from a position of rooted humility. He writes with the energies of most considerate love. He exhibits again what Christians have come to appreciate so much in Paul—the wedding of a brilliant and uncompromising intellect with a heart that is warmly and wonderfully kind.

So, chosen by God for this new life of love, dress in the wardrobe God picked out for you: compassion, kindness, humility, quiet strength, discipline. Be even-tempered, content with second place, quick to forgive an offense. Forgive as quickly and completely as the Master forgave you. And regardless of what else you put on, wear love. It's your basic, all-purpose garment. Never be without it. (Colossians 3:12-14)

1 & 2 THESSALONIANS

Taut and Joyful Expectancy

The way we conceive the future sculpts the present, gives contour and tone to nearly every action and thought through the day. If our sense of future is weak, we live listlessly. Much emotional and mental illness and most suicides occur among men and women who feel that they "have no future."

The Christian faith has always been characterized by a strong and focused sense of future, with belief in the Second Coming of Jesus as the most distinctive detail. From the day Jesus ascended into heaven, his followers lived in expectancy of his return. He told them he was coming back. They believed he was coming back. Paul wrote "with complete confidence,"

> We have the Master's word on it — that when the Master comes again to get us, those of us who are still alive will not get a jump on the dead and leave them behind. In actual fact, they'll be ahead of us. The Master himself will give the command. Archangel thunder! God's trumpet blast! He'll come down from heaven and the dead in Christ will rise — they'll go first. Then the rest of us who are still alive at the time will be caught up with them into the clouds to meet the Master. Oh, we'll be walking on air! And then there will be one huge family reunion with the Master. (1 Thessalonians 4:15-17)

They continue to believe it. For Christians, it is the most important thing to know and believe about the future.

The practical effect of this belief is to charge each moment of the present with hope. For if the future is dominated by the coming again of Jesus, there is little room left on the screen for projecting our anxieties and fantasies. It takes the clutter out of our lives. We're far more free to respond spontaneously to the freedom of God.

All the same, the belief can be misconceived so that it results in paralyzing fear for some, shiftless indolence in others. Paul's two letters to the Christians in Thessalonica, among much else, correct such debilitating misconceptions, prodding us to continue to live forward in taut and joyful expectancy for what God will do next in Jesus.

So, friends, take a firm stand, feet on the ground and head high. Keep a tight grip on what you were taught. . . . May Jesus himself and God our Father, who reached out in love and surprised you with gifts of unending help and confidence, put a fresh heart in you, invigorate your work, enliven your speech. (2 Thessalonians 2:15-17)

1 & 2 Timothy & Titus

Teach Believers with Your Life

Christians are quite serious in believing that when they gather together for worship and work, God is present and sovereign, really present and absolutely sovereign. God creates and guides, God saves and heals, God corrects and blesses, God calls and judges. With such comprehensive and personal leadership from God, what is the place of *human* leadership?

Quite obviously, it has to be second place. It must not elbow its way to the front, it must not bossily take over. Ego-centered, ego-prominent leadership betrays the Master. The best leadership in spiritual communities formed in the name of Jesus, the Messiah, is inconspicuous, not calling attention to itself but not sacrificing anything in the way of conviction and firmness either.

In his letters to two young associates — Timothy in Ephesus and Titus in Crete — we see Paul encouraging and guiding the development of just such leadership:

> *Teach believers with your life: by word, by demeanor, by love, by faith, by integrity. Stay at your post reading Scripture, giving counsel, teaching. . . . Cultivate these things. Immerse yourself in them. The people will all see you mature right before their eyes! Keep a firm grasp on both your character and your teaching. Don't be diverted. Just keep at it.*
> *(1 Timothy 4:11-13,15-16)*

What he had learned so thoroughly himself, he was now passing on, and showing them, in turn, how to develop a similar leadership in local congregations. "Your job," he told Titus, "is to speak out on the things that make for solid doctrine."

> *Guide older men into lives of temperance, dignity, and wisdom, into healthy faith, love, and endurance. Guide older women into lives of reverence so they end up as neither gossips nor drunks, but models of goodness. By looking at them, the younger women will know how to love their husbands and children, be virtuous and pure, keep a good house, be good wives. We don't want anyone looking down on God's Message because of their behavior. Also, guide the young men to live disciplined lives.*
>
> *But mostly, show them all this by doing it yourself, incorruptible in your teaching, your words solid and sane. (Titus 2:1-7)*

This is essential reading because ill-directed and badly formed spiritual leadership causes much damage in souls. Paul in both his life and his letters shows us how to do it right.

PHILEMON

A Ripple Effect

Every movement we make in response to God has a ripple effect, touching family, neighbors, friends, community. Belief in God alters our language. Love of God affects daily relationships. Hope in God enters into our work. Also their opposites — unbelief, indifference, and despair. None of these movements and responses, beliefs and prayers, gestures and searches, can be confined to the soul. They spill out and make history. If they don't, they are under suspicion of being fantasies at best, hypocrisies at worst.

Christians have always insisted on the historicity of Jesus — an actual birth, a datable death, a witnessed resurrection, locatable towns. There is a parallel historicity in the followers of Jesus. As they take in everything Jesus said and did — all of it a personal revelation of God in time and place — it all gets worked into local history, eventually into world history.

In his letter, Paul made a simple request of Philemon, a slave owner and fellow Christian: Take back — no, *welcome* back — your runaway slave Onesimus.

Here he is, hand-carrying this letter. . . ! He was useless to you before; now he's useful to both of us. I'm sending him back to you, but it feels like I'm cutting off my right arm in doing so. . . . You're getting him back now for good — and no mere slave this time, but a true Christian brother! . . .

So if you still consider me a comrade-in-arms, welcome him back as you would me. (Philemon 10-12,16-17)

Philemon and Onesimus had no idea that believing in Jesus would involve them in radical social change. But as the two of them were brought together by this letter, it did. And it still does.

HEBREWS

Live in Responsive Obedience

It seems odd to have to say so, but too much religion is a bad thing. We can't get too much of God, can't get too much faith and obedience, can't get too much love and worship. But *religion* — the well-intentioned efforts we make to "get it all together" for God — can very well get in the way of what God is doing for us. The main and central action is everywhere and always *what God has done, is doing, and will do for us.* Jesus is the revelation of that action. In fact, the writer of Hebrews says Jesus is "the centerpiece of everything we believe" (Hebrews 3:3). Our main and central task is to live in responsive obedience to God's action revealed in Jesus. Our part in the action is the act of faith.

But more often than not we become impatiently self-important along the way and decide to improve matters with our two cents' worth. We add on, we supplement, we embellish. But instead of improving on the purity and simplicity of Jesus, we dilute the purity, clutter the simplicity. We become fussily religious, or anxiously religious. We get in the way.

That's when it's time to read and pray our way through the letter to the Hebrews again, written for "too religious" Christians, for "Jesus-and" Christians. In the letter, it is Jesus-and-angels, or Jesus-and-Moses, or Jesus-and-priesthood. In our time it is more likely to be Jesus-and-politics, or Jesus-and-education, or even Jesus-and-Buddha. This letter deletes the hyphens, the add-ons. The writer urges us: "Don't be lured away from him by the latest speculations about him. The grace of Christ is the only good ground for life. Products named after Christ don't seem to do much for those who buy them" (Hebrews 13:9). Rather, "Keep your eyes on *Jesus*, who both began and finished this race we're in" (Hebrews 12:2). When we do that, the focus becomes clear and sharp again: God's action in Jesus. And we are free once more for the act of faith, the one human action in which we don't get *in* the way but *on* the Way.

JAMES

Deep and Living Wisdom

When Christian believers gather in churches, everything that can go wrong sooner or later does. Outsiders, on observing this, conclude that there is nothing to the religion business except, perhaps, business—and dishonest business at that. Insiders see it differently. Just as a hospital collects the sick under one roof and labels them as such, the church collects sinners. Many of the people outside the hospital are every bit as sick as the ones inside, but their illnesses are either undiagnosed or disguised. It's similar with sinners outside the church.

So Christian churches are not, as a rule, model communities of good behavior. They are, rather, places where human misbehavior is brought out in the open, faced, and dealt with.

The letter of James shows one of the church's early pastors skillfully going about his work of confronting, diagnosing, and dealing with areas of misbelief and misbehavior that had turned up in congregations committed to his care. Deep and living wisdom is on display here, wisdom both rare and essential. Wisdom is not primarily knowing the truth, although it certainly includes that; it is skill in living. For, what good is a truth if we don't know how to live it? What good is an intention if we can't sustain it?

> *Real wisdom, God's wisdom, begins with a holy life and is characterized by getting along with others. It is gentle and reasonable, overflowing with mercy and blessings, not hot one day and cold the next, not two-faced. You can develop a healthy, robust community that lives right with God and enjoy its results only if you do the hard work of getting along with each other, treating each other with dignity and honor.*
> *(James 3:17-18)*

According to church traditions, James carried the nickname "Old Camel Knees" because of thick calluses built up on his knees from many years of determined prayer. James lived what he wrote: "If you don't know what you're doing, pray to the Father. He loves to help. You'll get his help, and won't be condescended to when you ask for it. Ask boldly, believingly, without a second thought" (James 1:5-6). The prayer is foundational to the wisdom. Prayer is *always* foundational to wisdom.

1 & 2 Peter

A Breath of Fresh Air

Peter's concise confession — "You are the Messiah, the Christ" — focused the faith of the disciples on Jesus as God among us, in person, carrying out the eternal work of salvation. Peter seems to have been a natural leader, commanding the respect of his peers by sheer force of personality. In every listing of Jesus' disciples, Peter's name is invariably first.

In the early church, his influence was enormous and acknowledged by all. By virtue of his position, he was easily the most powerful figure in the Christian community. And his energetic preaching, ardent prayer, bold healing, and wise direction confirmed the trust placed in him.

The way Peter handled himself in that position of power is even more impressive than the power itself. He stayed out of the center, didn't "wield" power, maintained a scrupulous subordination to Jesus. Given his charismatic personality and well-deserved position at the head, he could easily have taken over, using the prominence of his association with Jesus to promote himself. That he didn't do it, given the frequency with which spiritual leaders do exactly that, is impressive. In fact, he told his readers to "be content with who you are, and don't put on airs. God's strong hand is on you; he'll promote you at the right time" (1 Peter 5:6). Peter is a breath of fresh air.

The two letters Peter wrote exhibit the qualities of Jesus that the Holy Spirit shaped in him: a readiness to embrace suffering rather than prestige, a wisdom developed from experience and not imposed from a book, a humility that lacked nothing in vigor or imagination. From what we know of the early stories of Peter, he had in him all the makings of a bully. That he didn't become a bully (and religious bullies are the worst kind) but rather the boldly confident and humbly self-effacing servant of Jesus Christ that we discern in these letters, is a compelling witness to what he himself describes as "a brand-new life, with everything to live for."

1, 2, & 3 JOHN

Wonderfully Explicit Direction

The two most difficult things to get straight in life are love and God. More often than not, the mess people make of their lives can be traced to failure or stupidity or meanness in one or both of these areas.

The basic and biblical Christian conviction is that the two subjects are intricately related. If we want to deal with God the right way, we have to learn to love the right way. If we want to love the right way, we have to deal with God the right way. God and love can't be separated: "Love means following his commandments, and his unifying commandment is that you conduct your lives in love" (2 John 5-6).

John's three letters provide wonderfully explicit direction in how this works. Jesus, the Messiah, is the focus: Jesus provides the full and true understanding of God; Jesus shows us the mature working-out of love. In Jesus, God and love are linked accurately, intricately, and indissolubly: "Everyone who confesses that Jesus is God's Son participates continuously in an intimate relationship with God. We know it so well, we've embraced it heart and soul, this love that comes from God" (1 John 4:15-16).

But there are always people around who don't want to be pinned down to the God Jesus reveals, to the love Jesus reveals. They want to make up their own idea of God, make up their own style of love. John was pastor to a church (or churches) disrupted by some of these people. In his letters we see him reestablishing the original and organic unity of God and love that comes to focus and becomes available to us in Jesus Christ.

JUDE

Fight with Everything You Have

Our spiritual communities are as susceptible to disease as our physical bodies. But it is easier to detect whatever is wrong in our stomachs and lungs than in our worship and witness. When our physical bodies are sick or damaged, the pain calls our attention to it, and we do something quick. But a dangerous, even deadly, virus in our spiritual communities can go undetected for a long time. As much as we need physicians for our bodies, we have even greater need for diagnosticians and healers of the spirit.

Jude's letter to an early community of Christians is just such diagnosis. He writes "insisting — begging! — that you fight with everything you have in you for this faith entrusted to us as a gift to guard and cherish" (Jude 3). It is all the more necessary in that those believers apparently didn't know anything was wrong, or at least not as desperately wrong as Jude points out.

There is far more, of course, to living in Christian community than protecting the faith against assault or subversion. Paranoia is as unhealthy spiritually as it is mentally. The primary Christian posture is, in Jude's words, "keeping your arms open and outstretched, ready for the mercy of our Master, Jesus Christ." All the same, energetic watchfulness is required. Jude encourages his readers to "carefully build yourselves up in this most holy faith by praying in the Holy Spirit, staying right at the center of God love" (Jude 20). Jude's whistle-blowing has prevented many a disaster.

REVELATION

Worship

The Bible ends with a flourish: vision and song, doom and deliverance, terror and triumph. The rush of color and sound, image and energy, leaves us reeling. But if we persist through the initial confusion and read on, we begin to pick up the rhythms, realize the connections, and find ourselves enlisted as participants in a multidimensional act of Christian worship.

It begins as the Four Animals chant night and day, never taking a break:

> *Holy, holy, holy*
> *Is God our Master, Sovereign-Strong*
> *THE WAS, THE IS, THE COMING. . . .*

> *Worthy, O Master! Yes, our God!*
> *Take the glory! the honor! the power!*
> *You created it all;*
> *It was created because you wanted it. (Revelation 4:8,11)*

Then the Twenty-four Elders join in, chanting their song. By the middle of this book, the "saved ones" stand together, singing the Song of Moses and the Song of the Lamb:

> *Mighty your acts and marvelous,*
>   *O God, the Sovereign-Strong!*

Righteous your ways and true,
    King of the nations!
Who can fail to fear you, God,
    give glory to your Name?
Because you and you only are holy,
    all nations will come and worship you,
        because they see your judgments are right. (Revelation 15:3-4)

John of Patmos, a pastor of the late first century, has worship on his mind, is preeminently concerned with worship. The vision, which is The Revelation, comes to him while he is at worship on a certain Sunday on the Mediterranean island of Patmos. He is responsible for a circuit of churches on the mainland whose primary task is worship. Worship shapes the human community in response to the living God. If worship is neglected or perverted, our communities fall into chaos or under tyranny.

Our times are not propitious for worship. The times never are. The world is hostile to worship. The Devil hates worship. As The Revelation makes clear, worship must be carried out under conditions decidedly uncongenial to it. Some Christians even get killed because they worship.

John's Revelation is not easy reading. Besides being a pastor, John is a poet, fond of metaphor and symbol, image and allusion, passionate in his desire to bring us into the presence of Jesus believing and adoring. But the demands he makes on our intelligence and imagination are well rewarded, for in keeping company with John, our worship of God will almost certainly deepen in urgency and joy.

Praise our God, all you his servants,
All you who fear him, small and great! (Revelation 19:5)

About the Author

EUGENE H. PETERSON is a writer, poet, and retired pastor. He has authored more than thirty-four books (not including *The Message*) and is a contributing editor for *Leadership*. He is Professor Emeritus of Spiritual Theology at Regent College in Vancouver, British Columbia. Eugene also founded Christ Our King Presbyterian Church in Bel Air, Maryland, where he ministered for twenty-nine years. He lives with his wife, Jan, in Montana.

Check Out These Other Message Titles from NavPress!

Conversations

Eugene Peterson
ISBN-13: 978-1-57683-959-1
ISBN-10: 1-57683-959-1

From *The Message* comes an entirely new way to experience God's Word. *Conversations* is a special annotated edition that features commentary from Eugene Peterson, one of today's most influential pastors and teachers. Filled with a wealth of insights, this study Bible enriches the text with notes from Peterson's own studies and sermons.

The Message Numbered Edition Personal Size

Eugene Peterson
ISBN-13: 978-1-60006-231-5
ISBN-10: 1-60006-231-8 Burgundy
ISBN-13: 978-1-60006-232-2
ISBN-10: 1-60006-232-6 Hardback

Improved style, size, and added study features make the completely redesigned *Message Numbered Edition* the contemporary translation of choice. These new features, combined with the everyday language of *The Message*, deliver a Bible-reading experience that is relatable, energetic, and amazingly fresh.

The Message//REMIX: Solo

Eugene Peterson
ISBN-13: 978-1-60006-105-9
ISBN-10: 1-60006-105-2

This innovative devotional is designed to change how you interact with God's Word. *The Message Remix: Solo* revolves around lectio divina, or "divine reading," an ancient approach to exploring Scripture updated for today's students. So don't just read the Bible. Get engaged with God's Word and let it revolutionize your life.

To order copies, visit your local Christian bookstore, call NavPress at
1-800-366-7788, or log on to www.navpress.com
To locate a Christian bookstore near you, call 1-800-991-7747.

Check Out These Other Message Titles from NavPress!

The Drive Time Message for Men – CDs 1 & 2

ISBN-13: 978-1-60006-071-7 CD 1
ISBN-10: 1-60006-071-4 CD 1

ISBN-13: 978-1-60006-142-4 CD 2
ISBN-10: 1-60006-142-7 CD 2

Devotions for Men on the Go. Before you open that first spreadsheet or place that first sales call, make sure you've had your time to reflect on what's most important in life. *Drive Time Message for Men* makes daily devotion simple. Featuring text from the best selling, *The Message* and only 5-7 minutes long, these audio devotions are perfect for your morning commute.

The Drive Time Message for Women – CDs 1 & 2

ISBN-13: 978-1-60006-072-4 CD 1
ISBN-10: 1-60006-072-2 CD 1

ISBN-13: 978-1-60006-143-1 CD 2
ISBN-10: 1-60006-143-5 CD 2

Is this how your day usually begins? Get everyone dressed, make breakfast, wrestle the kids into their car seats, try to back out the van without running over a scooter … and somehow, squeeze in a quiet time. *Drive Time Message for Women* makes daily devotion simple. Featuring text from the best-selling *The Message,* and only 5-7 minutes long, these audio devotions are perfect for your morning commute.

Check Out These Other Message Titles from NavPress!

My First Message

Eugene Peterson

ISBN-13: 978-1-57683-448-0
ISBN-10: 1-57683-448-4

A unique devotional Bible designed to encourage parent-child interaction, *My First Message* introduces children to God's Word through the best-selling *Message* Bible text, lively illustrations, short lessons, and a format that considers a small attention span. Much more than a storybook, it's an easy and fun way for parents to teach their children about God's Word and learn a lifelong devotional method.

Features include:

- A unique devotional Bible for children ages 4 to 8

- An illustrated design

- Each story designed to be read in 10-15 minutes

- Durable casebound cover

- Fun activities for parents and children